# COLONIAL WOMEN

# COLONIAL WOMEN

## Race and Culture in Stuart Drama

Heidi Hutner

OXFORD

UNIVERSITY PRESS

2001

# OXFORD
UNIVERSITY PRESS

Oxford   New York
Athens   Auckland   Bangkok   Bogotá   Buenos Aires
Cape Town   Chennai   Dar es Salaam   Delhi   Florence   Hong Kong   Istanbul
Karachi   Kolkata   Kuala Lumpur   Madrid   Melbourne   Mexico City   Mumbai
Nairobi   Paris   São Paulo   Shanghai   Singapore   Taipei   Tokyo   Toronto   Warsaw

and associated companies in
Berlin   Ibadan

Published by Oxford University Press, Inc.
198 Madison Avenue, New York, New York 10016

Oxford is a registered trademark of Oxford University Press, Inc.

Library of Congress Cataloging-in-Publication Data
Hutner, Heidi.
Colonial women : race and culture in stuart drama / Heidi Hutner.
p.   cm.
Includes bibliographical references and index.
ISBN 0-19-514188-1
1. English drama—17th century—History and criticism.   2. Women and literature—Great
Britain—History—17th century.   3. English drama—Restoration, 1660–1700—History and
criticism.   4. Women and Literature—Great Britain—Colonies—History.   5. Shakespeare,
William, 1564–1616. Tempest.   6. Behn, Aphra, 1640–1689. Widow ranter.   7. Land tenure
in literature.   8. Imperialism in Literature.   9. Colonies in literature.   10. Culture in
literature.   11. Women in literature.   12. Race in literature.   I. Title.
PR678.W6 H87 2001
822'.409352042—dc21      00-066547

1 3 5 7 9 8 6 4 2
Printed in the United States of America
on acid-free paper

For Olivia, K.F.,
S.R.H., and B.H.

# Acknowledgments

My deepest gratitude goes to Robert Markley, who has seen this project through its various stages—from dissertation to book. His extraordinary dedication has been unflagging over the years.

Many other teachers, colleagues, and friends have made this project possible. At the University of Washington, Carolyn Allen, Kate Cummings, Tom Lockwood, and Deborah C. Payne (of American University) saw me through the birth of the dissertation. They were astute readers of early versions of this study. Colleagues and friends at SUNY Stony Brook—Adrienne Munich, Helen Cooper, Tim Brennan, E. Ann Kaplan, Cliff Siskin, David Sheehan, Uschi Appelt, Eric Haralson, Steve Spector, Bruce Bashford, Ira Livingston, David Sheehan, Nancy Tomes, Peter Manning, and Lorenzo Simpson—have been extremely supportive throughout the writing and publication process. I am indebted to all of them.

I am grateful, as well, to the graduate students in my colonialism and literature seminar at SUNY Stony Brook. Their observations contributed to my thinking about colonialism, race, and gender. Sarah Lincoln, my graduate assistant, helped in important ways with the preparation of the manuscript.

At Oxford University Press, T. Susan Chang took initial interest in *Colonial Women*. I am thankful to her. Elissa Morris took over where Susan Chang left off, and she led the project to its final completion with the utmost of grace. She is a true professional.

No words can express my appreciation to Ken Fine for his steady encouragement and boundless belief in my writing and scholarship. His partnership in my life has made everything possible. I am forever grateful to the memory of my parents, Shirley and Bernard Hutner, for their inspirational devotion to and love of the arts, literature, and politics. And, finally, my inimitable toddler, Olivia, deserves a huge hug for granting me the time and space to complete this book.

# Contents

# COLONIAL WOMEN

# Introduction

## *Colonial Women and Stuart Drama*

In seventeenth-century accounts of English expansion and colonization, the native woman is presented as a symbol of the New World. Her body is identified with the land and its native inhabitants: she is at once terrifying and beautiful, dangerous and nurturing.[1] The explorer, colonist, or travel writer is almost always male, and the land that he surveys and conquers is a feminized Eve, as Mary Louise Pratt writes, "whom he in his unobjectionable way plunders and possesses."[2] In this study, I shall suggest that in the dramatic literature of the seventeenth century, English patriarchal culture attempts to define and, for English Royalists after 1660, restore itself over the body of the native woman or the European woman who has gone native. In the drama, as in historical accounts, the symbol of the native woman is used to justify and promote the success of the English appropriation, commodification, and exploitation of the New World and its native inhabitants. In crucial ways, then, the figure of the native woman functions as a means of cultural self-definition for the English. The seduction of the native woman, in this respect, is a symbolic strategy to stabilize the turbulent sociopolitical and religious conflicts in Restoration England under the inclusive ideology of colonial expansion and profit. The native woman operates discursively in travel accounts and histories of the period as a means to bring order to England's unstable world, and the seventeenth-century stage dramatizes this image repeatedly in an anxiety-laden reestablishment of patriarchal identity by the dramatic spectacle of the native woman falling for her European seducer/exploiter. Examining the ways in which the native woman is represented will deepen and enhance our understanding of the conflicted ideological strategies at work during the Restoration—England's first major period of imperial and colonial expansion—as well as expand our understanding of the interpenetrating discourses of gender and race in the politics of English literary history.[3]

The repression and regulation of the native woman is enacted within the romance narrative—the model through which disorderly European women are traditionally subordinated in seventeenth-century literature. Natalie Zemon Davis argues that woman, in early modern Europe, represented social disorder "par excellence." It is through female subordination, Davis argues, that social order and patriarchal authority are symbolically maintained: "[i]n the little world of the family, with its conspicuous tension between intimacy and power, the larger matters of political and social order could find ready symbolization."[4] In this study, I want to add to Davis's argument the category of "race" and its intersections with gender in my analysis of colonial discourse and the drama of the seventeenth century. The domination of the New World is dramatized through the tale of the native woman who falls in love with the white man and willingly gives herself to him and converts to Christianity. In giving herself to her white lover, her "savage" culture is justifiably dominated and tamed by the Englishman. Moreover, in dominating the native woman, the English colonizer not only "saves" the heathen by Christianizing and civilizing her, but guards himself against becoming a rebellious and chaotic other. In "saving" her, he restores and "saves" himself.[5]

In the seventeenth-century plays that I examine, English playwrights construct dramatic representations of the other—not only as a means to dominate and domesticate the other, but also as a means to discipline, order, and structure England's own systems of knowledge and social organization.[6] Hayden White asserts that cultures in crisis define themselves by pointing "to something in the landscape which is manifestly different from" themselves. "If we do not know what we think 'civilization' is," White suggests, "we can always find an example of what it is not."[7] During the Restoration, as Earl Miner argues, the "staging" of the wild New World allowed the English to play out their sociopolitical struggles and to attempt to stabilize their own "topsy turvy" world.[8]

Important critical work has begun on women and colonial discourse in English literature of the seventeenth and eighteenth centuries by Ania Loomba, Kim Hall, Margo Hendricks, Patricia Parker, Margaret Ferguson, Laura Brown, Felicity Nussbaum, Charlotte Sussman, Moira Ferguson, Bridget Orr, Joseph Roach, and Srinivas Aravamudan, among others—and I will draw on their analyses and theories throughout this study.[9] However, other than Orr's *Empire on the English Stage, 1660–1714*, which takes a broad look at English imperialism in a dramatic context, there exists scant criticism on colonialism, gender, and Restoration drama.[10] More investigations into the problematic of race and gender in Stuart drama needs to be done, therefore, and this study seeks to help fill that gap by demonstrating the importance of the figure of the colonized woman as she is represented on the seventeenth-century English stage.

*Colonial Women* focuses primarily on intersections of race and gender on the Restoration stage and in English Restoration society and culture, but begins in the early seventeenth century for two reasons. It was during the early seventeenth century that Virginia, England's first successful colony, was founded, and Restoration writers drew extensively on the historical and literary accounts of this period to depict colonialism. Virginia was a royal colony; the Massachusetts Bay Colony was associated with Puritanism and dissent, thus Restoration writers (and early Stuart dramatists) were politically drawn to look to Virginia for its settings. As Nicholas Jose argues, the literature of the Restoration looks nostalgically backward to the pre–civil war era as a time when England was supposedly more politically stable.[11] A full examination of Restoration literary culture, therefore, demands an account of the historical events that preceded it—specifically, England's efforts in the seventeenth century to establish profitable colonies in North America. This work links literature and history because, as Laura Brown argues, it is impossible to write a critique of the literature of the Restoration without taking into account the implications of questions of empire in England's history.[12] The late seventeenth century was the period of England's development of its first major overseas empire, the primary phase of the slave trade, as well as a period of extreme political and ideological turbulence in England. Colonial expansion and empire building were viewed by many English dramatists as a means to stabilize and unite the divided nation. An examination of Restoration drama, then, requires not only the linking of history and literature, but also investigating the intercultural relationships of England and its first successful colonies. *Colonial Women* demonstrates how the spectacle of expansion can become a means to allow us to understand the socio-ideological significance of the other woman.

The dramatic portrayal of the New World as a submissive and willing female body assuages white masculinist anxieties about colonization, about the exploitability of America for its resources, about women, and about the stability of patriarchal authority. Carolyn Merchant suggests that the view of the New World as feminine is conditioned by the belief in early modern Europe that nature was female. She points out that, while prior to the sixteenth century nature had been viewed as the fertile, abundant mother, during the sixteenth and seventeenth centuries, there was a growing tendency to perceive this feminized nature as a disordered and unproductive wilderness that needed to be tamed and controlled. Eve was associated with the expulsion from Eden into the evil wilderness, and "it was the perception of nature as wilderness that became important in the early modern era. For Protestants such as John

Locke, John Calvin, and the New England Puritans, God had authorized human dominion over earth."[13] Just as nature came to be viewed as disordered and wild during the seventeenth century, so, too, women and indigenous people in the New World were feminized—regarded as children or dependents who needed to be guarded or controlled.[14] The construction of woman and nature as wild and disorderly promoted a hierarchical class structure of society, with the upper-class male at the intellectual head, and woman and others—such as the lower classes and native people—as the bodies that assist him.[15] The ideological construction of both woman and nature as chaotic and savage justified English economic motivations for the exploitation of the land and people of the New World.

The view of the New World as an indigenous woman needing to be taken and tamed by a white male European lover can be seen throughout early travel narratives and art in the woman-as-land metaphor, such as Christopher Columbus's (1492) discovery that the earth is shaped like a "pear," with a "protuberance" at its "highest" point with "something like a woman's nipple." Jan van der Straet's famous drawing (ca. 1575) portrays the European male's discovery of America as a sexualized meeting between Vespucci and a native woman. Samuel Eliot Morison describes how, for the Spanish, "the New World gracefully yielded her virginity to the conquering Castilians." In "Guiana carmen Epicum" (1596), George Chapman suggests that the female Guiana "whose rich feete are mines of golde,/Whose forehead knockes against the roofe of Starres," stands on tiptoe looking at beautiful England, with "every signe of all submission making" toward the English. Sir Walter Ralegh (1596) writes that, "Guiana is a countrey that hath yet her maydenhead" and she waits for the English colonizers to put "their glad feet on smooth Guianas brest."[16] In European depictions of the New World, as these examples demonstrate, the land of the New World is feminized and sexualized, and the indigenous woman invites her own appropriation and domestication.[17]

Annette Kolodny attributes the woman-as-land metaphor to the "need to experience land as a nurturing, giving maternal breast because of the threatening, alien, and potentially emasculating terror of the unknown. . . . In a sense, to make the new continent Woman was already to civilize it a bit, casting the stamp of human relations upon what was otherwise unknown and untamed."[18] Anne McClintock suggests "the feminizing of terra incognita . . . betrays acute paranoia and a . . . sense of male anxiety and boundary loss."[19] It is thus the fear of, as well as the desire for, the New World which leads male explorers and colonizers to "civilize" the land by marking her as woman. The woman-as-land metaphor is portrayed ambivalently by Europeans in the seventeenth century: she is seductive, beautiful, alluring, and threatening, dark, unknown and potentially cannibalistic. While the white colonist is drawn to her beauty and natural resources, there is a persistent fear of engulfment and loss of self for the white male in their encounter.

The Malinche and Pochahontas myths, which I discuss at length in later chapters, are also crucial to dramatic representations of the woman-as-land metaphor and interracially gendered contact in the seventeenth century. Malinche and Pochahontas demonstrate how women, in McClintock's words, "served as boundary markers of imperialism, the ambiguous mediators of what appeared to be . . . the male agon of empire."[20] Although Malinche's tale takes place in a Spanish colonial context more than one hundred years before Pocahontas's contact with the English, seventeenth-century narratives and dramatic texts certainly drew on it (in the case of Dryden and Howard, they drew on it directly, see chapter 3). For seventeenth-century dramatists, Malinche and Pocahontas both figure as symbols of the native woman who is willingly conquered and exploited by the European lover/colonizer.

Malinche was an indigenous noblewoman sold into slavery by her parents, and she was afterward given to Cortes as a gift by a tribe he defeated soon after his arrival in Mexico. Malinche became Cortes's translator and lover, and she bore him a son. Later she married one of Cortes's generals. Malinche assisted Cortes throughout his imperial travels in the Mexican territory and supposedly contributed to the success of his project. Cortes's contemporaries give Malinche substantial credit for the colonization of Mexico. Malinche, then, performs as a sign of the easy accommodation and acculturation of the New World to the Old. Further, as a native woman colonized by the *Spanish*, she becomes a safe fantasy figure for English dramatists to graft their fears of and longings for miscegenation on and an easy target to impose their anti-Spanish biases against.

The myth of Pocahontas draws on the Malinche tale as well as the imagery of the New World as a feminized land waiting, wanting, and needing to be conquered.[21] Pocahontas assisted Captain John Smith in the early stages of the colony by saving his life, bringing the colonists much needed food, and warning them of impending Indian attacks. Several years after Smith left Virginia, Pocahontas was kidnapped by the colonists. At this time she learned English, was baptized and renamed Rebecka, and married John Rolfe—the first successful tobacco planter. Pocahontas thus symbolizes both Virginia's establishment and its economic success.

The functional differences between the Malinche and Pochahontas stories demonstrate the ambivalence of English attitudes toward interracial relationships with Native American women. In both tales, women act as intermediaries between European colonizers and Indians; they are represented as saviors, lovers, and peacemakers. For the Spanish in Mexico, intermarriage is encouraged. As Gary Nash writes, "[b]ecause the Indians supplied the bulk of the labor for colonial extractive and productive enterprises in the early decades, it was not only desirable but necessary to assimilate them into the European culture." After the initial extreme periods of violence passed and the Indians were thoroughly subordinated, the native peoples were no longer seen as a threat to the Spanish colonists and "an impressive degree of acculturation and assimilation" took place.[22] The thousands of Indian women who became wives, concubines, and mistresses to the Spaniards made this assimilation possible, and their acculturation depended on the sexual domination of the Spanish colonists. Malinche's story of interracial romance was repeated by thousands of Indian women in Mexico.[23]

Intermarriage with Native Americans in colonial Virginia and other North American English colonies, on the other hand, was not encouraged for the most part, except in unusual instances.[24] Pocahontas's story, or rather its ambivalent and repeated recasting in dramatic texts, thus reflects English colonists' fear of interracial contact as the seventeenth century progressed. Robert S. Tilton asserts that in the early phases of the Virginia colony, miscegenation was believed to hold the potential for the peaceful acquisition of land and property and for controlling of indigenous people, but it was also seen as an unnatural act and was frowned upon by white society. Tilton argues that the marriage of Pocahontas and Rolfe "came to be seen as a model that, to the detriment of both Indians and whites, had not been followed during the earliest years of the English colonial enterprise. It was interpreted as proof that the merging of the two peoples and cultures was, or at least had been possible."[25] Nash attributes the English discouragement of intermarriage with Native Americans to economic greed. Unlike in Mexico, where the Spaniards were able to subdue and enslave the Indians with military force, Indians in the North American coastal territories could not be forced to supply labor (except in South Carolina in the late seventeenth century) because the English did not have the military strength of the Spaniards. As the century progressed, trade with the Indians became of negligible economic importance, and by the 1620s tobacco dominated the Virginia economy, and Indian land became the most coveted commodity. After the 1622 massacre—which was mostly about English encroachment on Indian territories—"apartheid" plans against the Indians replaced those of acculturation.[26]

White male fears about the threat of the feminized people and land which resist acculturation in the New World disrupt colonial narratives and colonial dramas throughout the seventeenth century. Indeed, I would argue, the woman-as-land metaphor and the romantic myths of Malinche and Pocahontas are used in both historical narratives and the drama of the period to mystify the highly vexed story of power and desire in gender and racial relations. Lurking beneath the surface of these stories are crucial yet often neglected records of powerful Indian women from the Algonkian North American Coastal groups who greatly threatened English colonial culture in the early contact period.

Before delving into the history of the Coastal Algonkians,[27] I want to emphasize that most of what we know of seventeenth-century North American Indians comes from the records of European men. Paula Gunn Allen aptly states that, "[a]ny original documentation that exists [about Native Americans] is buried under the flood of readily available, published material written from the colonizer's patriarchal perspective, almost all of which is based on the white man's belief in universal male dominance."[28] In a well-known essay, Gayatri Spivak asserts that in the "context of colonial production, the subaltern has no history and cannot speak, [and] the subaltern as female is even more deeply in shadow."[29] The Algonkians, moreover, were not a literate people, so most of what we know has come from European records. These records are obviously partial, skewed toward very particular political, economic, and social aims. While I will try to offer a more complete picture of seventeenth-century North American Native American women and their cultures, sources for this period are extremely limited, and, as a middle-class white Jewish American woman, what I write must be filtered (however reluctantly) through yet another subjective and/or ideological lens.

In general, as Allen notes, North American tribal cultures are "never patriarchal." They are "woman-centered"—what Allen calls "gynocratic." According to Allen, the destruction of the North American tribes resulted in part from the European fear of gynocracy. The powerful positions of women in Native American cultures threatened the European patriarchal order: "[w]ives telling husbands and brothers whether to buy or sell an item, daughters telling fathers whom they could and could not murder, empresses attending parleys with colonizers and being treated with deference by male leaders did not sit well with the invaders." Since the early 1500s, European invaders made every attempt to obliterate all records of woman-centered societies and social systems in North America, so that "no American and few American Indians would remember that gynocracy was the primary social order of Indian America prior to 1800." The male colonists' need to dominate the Indian woman—to stamp out gynocracy—stemmed from the knowledge that "as long as women held unquestioned power of such magnitude, attempts at total conquest of the continents were bound to fail."[30]

Robert Steven Grumet suggests that throughout the seventeenth century in North America, "Coastal Algonkians managed to maintain an independent existence in the midst of a pervasive and often hostile European presence." The "persistence of native cultural forms" is especially evident "in the continuing importance of women in Coastal Algonkian society during the seventeenth and eighteenth centuries."[31] Women were a significant part of the political and social structure of Alquonkian societies. They were leaders, hunters, healers, matchmakers, house builders, agriculturalists, and shamans.

Indeed, there were many powerful female leaders in the seventeenth century among the North American Coastal tribes. In 1607, John Smith described the Queene of Appamatuck, the elder sister of Wahunsunacock, who was the "paramount sachem of Powhatan confederacy." Significantly, Smith burned her village in 1610. George Fox, the founder of Quakerism, wrote of " 'the old Empress [of Accomack who] . . . sat in council' " during his visit to Maryland in 1673. In 1705, Robert Beverley spoke of " 'Pungoteque, Govern'd by a Queen, but a small nation' " and " 'Nanduye. A Seat of the Empress. Not above 20 Families, but she hath all the Nations of this shore under Tribute.' "[32] These Native American women functioned in vital and crucial ways to their tribes and culture.

There was also a "squa-sachim of Puckanokick" who ruled the constituent groups of the Massachussetts confederacy, but "she was forced to align herself with the English, and records show that she continually sold land to the colonists and represented their interests in native diplomacy up to her death in 1667." The Narragansett sunksquaw Quaipan (also known as Magnus and Matantuck) was the sister of Niantic sachem Ninigret, married to Mexanno, son of Narragansett leader Canonicus. She was first known in 1667 after she sent 300 warriors to fight against the "interior Nipmuck for defying her authority." Although Narragansett counseled the Wampanoag against warring against the English, when the colonists attacked the main Narragansett fortress, Quaipan fought against the English and was killed by them in the spring of 1676 in King Philip's war.[33]

Ethnographic records also discuss a Pocasset sunksquaw named Weetamoo, the widow of Wampanoag sachem Alexander, brother of King Philip who died in 1662. She later married Ninigret's son Quinnipin, and her sister became the spouse of King Philip. Weetamoo was King Philip's ally soon after the conflict began, and she "served as a war chief commanding over 300 warriors." Weetamoo's troops eventually diminished to thirty and she finally drowned in a swamp in an attempt to escape to the interior in August 1676. Awashonks, another sister of Ninigret, became squaw sachem of the Sakonnet tribe of the Wampanoag confederation sometime before July 24, 1671, when they submitted to the English. She submitted in opposition to her brother's (a Sakonnet under-sachem) wish that they not give up their firearms. Awashonks sold a portion of the Sakonnet territory to the English in 1673, and "[s]he received a Wampanoag war embassy in early 1675."[34] Awashonks chose a neutral position in the conflict, but because of "English aggression and her people's desire for revenge," she was forced to enter the war in late 1675. She "led her people against the English until forced to surrender in May, 1676. Instrumental in convincing many of her warriors to then side with the English, Awashonks thus saved her followers from deportation into slavery to the West Indies, a fate met by many of the native belligerents at the close of King Philip's War in 1676." Other late seventeenth-century women sachem include Mamanuch-qua, and Mamareoktke and Mamaprocht of the Esopus,[35] as well as the Queen of the Pamunkey who will be discussed in depth in chapter 4.

Women played other powerful roles in Algonkian societies. They were shamans, herbalists, witches, and healers, and other than in the Chesapeake area where priesthoods were instituted and the social structure was most stratified, women shamans were considered to be extremely influential in their societies. These roles were especially important as political leaders needed the sanctions of shamans to gain the support of followers. Women shamans were considered particularly powerful because they were believed to embody both male and female spirits.[36]

Among the Algonkian groups (other than those of the Chesapeake area), there was an egalitarian mode of production and an egalitarian sociopolitical structure, and work divisions such as hunting and agriculture became less defined as people aged. Also, both sexes could and did work at different tasks according to the community's needs.[37] All major activities were undertaken cooperatively, such as deer drives, the setting of deer trappings, house building, fishing, shell fishing, and wild-plant gathering. Small game hunting was performed competently by both sexes. Women played significant roles in "both the domestic modes of production and in foreign trade" as well. In addition, the "disposition of goods of Coastal Algonkian society" was egalitarian, as "the production of each spouse [was] the property of the other." Finally, it must be noted that there were five political levels in Algonkian society: the clan, the village, the district, the tribe, and the confederacy. At the clan and village (the "primary international agent of Algonkian society") levels especially, all domestic affairs were regulated matrilineally and matri-locally.[38]

Among the Chesapeake, however, Chief Powhatan asserted a far more strat-ified patriarchal authority.[39] He married a hundred women from villages throughout his region and controlled several Indian tribes by limiting commercial activity and encouraging intermarriage with his children. Kathleen M. Brown suggests that the decrease in female authority among the Powhatans in the seventeenth century stemmed from contact with the English. As hostilities mounted between the two groups, and military force became increasingly important to the survival of the Indians, the patriarchal tendencies of the Virginia Algonkian groups probably intensified. Thus, during the first twenty years of contact with the English, Indian women lost some of their power among the

Virginia Algonkians.[40] Other than in the Chesapeake area, however, Algonkian women wielded a great deal of authority. Yet, as Brown argues, even the female Virginia Algonkians, "were perhaps more powerful in their subordination than English women."[41]

I want to suggest that these Coastal Algonkian matrilineal and matrifocal cultures greatly threatened the cultural and political values of English male self-definitions in the early contact period. English anxieties about the instability of patriarchal authority were already intensely heightened throughout the seventeenth century, and the discovery of Alongkian gynocracies and women-centered Indian cultures further aggravated these fears and fed the need to represent the Native American women, in travel narratives and in dramatic texts, as submissive, passive, and traditionally sexualized—in effect, to repress the history of the Native American woman as politically, socially, and economically central to her society.

Crucial, as well, to the portrait of the indigenous woman and interracial romance in the drama of the seventeenth century are the histories of seventeenth-century white women in the colonial context. In a number of the plays examined in the following chapters, for instance, European gender roles are consolidated through a separation of white women from Indian women and women of African descent. In the drama, white women are pitted against Indian and black women in a binary of domesticity versus wildness. Indeed, white women who do not conform to traditionally subordinated roles are depicted as going native. African and Indian women are symbolically linked in seventeenth-century historical and dramatic texts—they are often mutually constituted as chaotic, libidinous, sinful, evil, and out of control.[42]

As Brown demonstrates, categories of gender and race were integrally bound at this time: "Virginia was claimed by England and settled . . . at the same historical moment in which the English state, merchants, and adventurers had intensified their commitment to patriarchal households and female domesticity as the defining characteristics of Englishness."[43] Thus the family, with its strong father and good wife, functioned as the model through which patriarchy could be maintained. English women who overstepped the boundaries of male authority were viewed as scolds, shrews, and witches, and were contrasted with the "[q]uiet, pious, hardworking" wife who could "facilitate community order [by] compelling men to fulfill their patriarchal responsibilities."[44] The Virginia colonists, in particular, tried to recreate the socioeconomic conditions of England in the New World.[45] In effect, the view of the English man taming the female New World fused with English gender discourses at home and served as "a powerful justification for English domination" of America and its native peoples.[46]

As the seventeenth century progressed in Virginia, the ideal of the domestic white wife became integrally linked to racial distinctions. An increasing number of attempts were made to control English women's sexuality through more severe punishment for bastardy and extramarital and, especially, interracial sex. Before 1662, interracial sex was treated criminally in much the same way as same-race extramarital sex.[47] After 1662, interracial sex, for white women, was no longer tolerated. In 1662, the Virginia assembly passed two measures: the first declared that children of slaves should follow the mother's condition, the second made fornication between the races illegal. In 1691, Virginia legislators reinforced the ban against white women's engagement in interracial sex in a new statute that declared the danger in the "abominable mixture and spurious issue which hereafter may encrease in this dominion, as well by negroes, mulattoes, and Indians intermarrying with English, or other white women." The legislators further asserted,

Whatsoever English or other white man or woman being free shall intermarry with a negroe, mulatto, or Indian man or woman bond or free shall within three months after such marriage be banished and removed from this dominion forever.[48]

The legislation indicated particularly severe punishments for white English women who gave birth to illegitimate children by men of African descent. The children of such unions were punished severely as well. Thus the 1662 and 1691 Virginia legislation forced white women into the racial divide.[49] In the last third of the seventeenth century, then, racial distinctions were made, in large measure, by attempting to control white female sexuality.

As these laws demonstrate, seventeenth-century English women could not be contained and controlled—at least not absolutely—and gender categories "blurred dangerously" between the good wife and the bad, the sexually promiscuous and the virginal, and traditional roles of male and female.[50] The possession and regulation of a domesticated white wife in the English colony represented an ideal that few men could achieve. English men continued to outnumber white women until the last third of the century in Virginia; men who came as indentured servants rarely moved up the social scale;[51] and English women resisted male control on various levels—as servants their sexuality failed to be regulated, as wives they "gossiped" and they thus assumed a political voice in social matters.[52] The cultural desire to control English women, and the impossibility of achieving this goal, therefore, leads to the endless admonition of white women who go native in colonial dramatic contexts.

African women are far less visible onstage than either white or Indian women in Stuart drama, yet their feared presence, as in Shakespeare's *Tempest* and Thomas Southerne's *Oroonoko*, forms an important backdrop to the functions of gender and race in the colonial performance. In seventeenth-century Virginia, as Brown demonstrates, black women (even more so than Indian women who could not be forced to labor but lived on coveted land) fulfill a vital economic function—as agricultural laborers and as the bearers of future slave laborers. They filled the places of white indentured servants (slavery eventually replaced indentured servitude altogether) who labored in the to-bacco fields and thus allowed white women to function as traditional domestic wives. By the 1660s, African women outnumbered white women in several counties, and they outnumbered Indian servants for most of the century.[53] The act of 1662 (perpetual bondage for slave children), as I discussed above, distinguished African mothers from English mothers. The 1667 act which marked "Negro" people as separate from Christians further distanced white and African women.[54] Although interracial fornication was illegal after 1691, white men were immune from punishment. This testifies to the function of women of African descent in mid- to late-seventeenth-century white colonial culture—their bodies did not legally threaten male property rights because black women's slave children were not viewed as the heirs of white men, but rather as property belonging to the slaveholders (white women's mixed race children were not born slaves). Yet, conversely, as Lynda E. Boose points out, because the white man's seed of inheritance (property, name, authority) is "wasted" in interracial sexual contact with the black woman, she potentially destroys the European patriarchal social order, by "swallow[ing] up" the political system "within the signification of her body."[55]

Nash suggests that African slave women were regarded particularly negatively by English men because they arrived in greatest numbers in North America just when the disparity among white males and females was nearly leveled. Had there been fewer white women, he argues, "the alleged distaste for dark skinned partners would doubtlessly have broken down." For example, in Barbados, Jamaica, and the Leeward Islands, where English women were scarce, English men eagerly followed the practice of the Spanish and Portuguese, living with and sometimes marrying their female slaves. To outlaw sexual relations with women of African descent in most English Caribbean colonies would have been impossible. In effect, "[where] white women were absent, black women were needed; where they were needed, they were enthusiastically accepted and laws prohibiting interracial sex and marriage never passed."[56]

I want to suggest that the unrepresentable black women in the seventeenth-century colonial stage, with its emphasis on the Virginia plantation version of colonialism, rests ambivalently on an axis of desire and aversion; she is enmeshed in an emerging slave economy of trade where profit permeates and eventually dominates English concepts of heredity. Interracial sexual contact with the black woman produces more profit, but it also produces mulatto children who are of white as well as of African descent. These slave children (not heirs) and their mothers are unrepresentable because they serve as a reminder of forbidden desire, of loss, of absence, of human brutality that must be denied, forgotten, or explained away.

In the colonial and dramatic history of the seventeenth century, then, the defining of a male sexual and political identity rests on the repression of the native woman, the effacement of the black woman, and the regulation of European women's sexuality. Black women enable white women to function as domestic ideals, as black female slaves fulfill white women's former roles as indentured agricultural laborers. Native women are justifiably dominated as trade with Indians becomes of less economic value and as Indian land grows increasingly coveted in a tobacco economy. Since Indians in the English North American colonies could not be subdued into slavery (for the most part), their destruction—not assimilation—was necessary to achieve the colonists' economic expansionist ends. In seventeenth-century drama, the histories of African and Indian women play themselves out in the visual and physical absence of black and Indian female characters and the idealized tragi-romantic versions of the Malinche and Pocahontas stories—which deny native women's power. Yet the feared presence of the Algonkian gynocracies, uncontrollable (even if visually absent) African women, and unruly white women subvert the colonialist patriarchal order again and again. The English men's yearning for interracial sexual contact and the resistance of rebellious English women at home and in the New World testify to the ambiguous web of gender, race, and economic relations in the dramatic history of colonial expansion.

The woman-as-land metaphor and the colonial romance narrative, therefore, remain unstable signs for the imperialist enterprise in the seventeenth century because the native woman, the English woman, and the woman of African descent cannot be fully contained. As Homi K. Bhabha suggests, colonization is a dialectical process, whereby alterity potentially destabilizes the dominant discourse of the colonizer.[57] Moreover, the *"ambivalence"* of the colonial stereotype gives it "currency" and "ensures its repeatability."[58] The ambivalent sign of native woman in the New World, therefore, is endlessly restaged and reformulated throughout the seventeenth century in an attempt to repress the dangers of what cannot be contained. In the dramatic texts examined in the following chapters, powerful colonial women constantly threaten to overpower and destroy patriarchal authority and the white male European lover or husband. The disorderly and seductive woman-as-land metaphor thus represents

what the white male cannot control within himself (or his white female counterpart): the native woman is a symbol of the sexually lascivious other he/she
may potentially become.[59]

The effort to control disorderly white women (women gone native) in the
drama becomes more intensified over the century; in Shakespeare's *Tempest*
(chapter 1), for example, Miranda remains "pure" and within her father's
power, but as the century progresses, white female characters in the drama
take on negative stereotypical characteristics of native women to varying de-
grees. However, it must be remembered that such representational slippage
between native and white women is situational: playwrights alter their por-
trayals as the need arises. The connections between the literary texts (Renaissance island plays and Restoration apologetics for imperial ambition) and historical material (eastern tribes) are going to be of a different order by the late
seventeenth century for two reasons: there is a much wider cultural and social
divide to bridge in dramatizing non-European peoples when the English colonial project in North America is just underway; and by the 1680s, the understanding of the history of European-Indian relations has undergone significant transformation. Thus, in *The Widow Ranter* (chapter 4), Aphra Behn can
draw on a wider variety of resources than Shakespeare; she has half a century
of English colonial discourse to consider, not to mention various stage por-
trayals of non-European peoples by Dryden, Howard, Fletcher, Settle, and
Davenant.

In *Cities of the Dead*, Joseph Roach describes performance as "the doomed
search for originals [which] continuously audition[s] stand-ins. . . . Performance . . . stands in for an elusive entity that it is not but that it must vainly
aspire both to embody and replace."[60] The search for nostalgic originals, then,
occurs in a process of "surrogation[,] . . . the three sided relationship of memory, performance, and subsitution" which rarely, if ever, succeeds. The imprecise fit of surrogation causes a range of anxieties, from "sentimentalism to
raging paranoia."[61] Thus, stable meaning is impossible to achieve in the theater, as performance is often destabilized by the distance or slippage between
the body of the actor and the character being played.[62] I want to suggest that
the slippage between signifier and signified of the actor/character in the drama
is even more greatly exaggerated when it comes to playing the other *woman*.
For Shakespeare and Fletcher, there were no actresses on the stage; for Restoration playwrights, women could play women, but women could not wear
black face. The other woman looked white, yet she was supposed to be of
color (but was she/was she not?).

To put it bluntly, in both the early and late seventeenth century, when white
people played Indians, audiences were always being reminded of the fiction
being deployed. Dramatists were simultaneously enunciating and erasing, call-

ing attention to and denying, iconizing and debasing, interracial contact and erotic desire for the other woman. In the plays I analyze in *Colonial Women*, therefore, the anxiety about performing the Native American woman or woman of African descent is addressed anxiously in disturbing and complicated ways—through longing, absence, parody, death. I want to suggest that the impossibility of playing the other woman without slippage, without irony, without oscillation of identity, reflects and reproduces a whole host of social fears about interracial contact, empire building, slavery, and the mistreatment of Native American and African peoples.

The drama presents, on the one hand, an idealized, sanitized, and self-contained version of colonization. What Timothy Murray calls, in a different context, a "theatrical legitimation . . . [which is in part] the combined process of historical and contemporary reception[,]" whereby "the allegorical re-positioning or re-generation of objects and Subjects through narration" creates an *"allegorical transference."* This complex theatrical process of legitimating both the theatrical performance and the sociocultural discourses which produce and are produced by the spectacle, create a fiction of representational truth and "sanction institutional authority."[63] The colonial drama, as this study will show, legitimates and sanctions its own literary and performative codes. By recreating their versions of the native woman-as-land on the English stage, dramatists such as Shakespeare, Fletcher, Duffet, Durfey, Dryden, and Behn, among others, present the colonial project as a justifiable repression of the native woman in a safe setting—the English theater—where audiences may be observers of both the exotic and the familiar at the same time. In the stage performance, one could view the sights and hear the sounds of English distillations of the New World, marry the native princess, possess her people and land, and gain enormous wealth and power, all without leaving the comforts of the theater. These plays, then, might be perceived as safe and sanitized versions of colonization because the Native American, black, and white women gone native were only acting their parts. These actresses (or actors, in the case of early Stuart drama) might not appear to threaten the male observer in the dramatic context in England because the real natives lived, for the most part, thousands of miles away and because they became proper for the drama *after* the fact, *after* the threat they posed was at least partially eradicated.

Yet the drama also serves as a flawed means of surveillance and control. Susan J. Owen explains how Restoration drama functions as a "[t]heatre of [c]ontradiction," which exposes the social fractures and political divisions in Restoration society.[64] Robert Markley suggests that drama functions "as both performance and conflict—as fiction and substance—in historical transformations of language and culture."[65] I would argue that the contradictory and conflicted nature of the stage text in performance during this period destabilizes the spectacular attempt to legitimate the colonial project. Crucial to the fear of the native woman and her culture is the concern of the English going native, especially white English women—and that is precisely what these players do (however imperfectly). Is it not ironic that the stage itself in the Restoration, and especially its actresses, is associated with sexual wildness and chaos, the very social conditions for which the native women and women of African descent are deemed heathens?[66] And while in many of the plays examined in this work Indian and African women are replaced by white female characters (stand-ins), this substitution produces a myriad of crises. Over and over, white female characters take on the stereotypical characteristics of native female chaos and patriarchal colonial authority is severely, if temporarily, threatened. As the following chapters will demonstrate, specters of the Indian holocaust and ghosts of the enslaved, murdered, and brutalized Africans haunt these plots and the white characters who are supposedly the embodiments of European civilized virtue. Thus, the double desire to possess the New World and keep its people at a distance and the fear that neither can be accomplished leads to the repeated restaging of the woman-as-land metaphor as both a celebration and a compensatory fiction.

Chapter 1 looks first at the Pocahontas myth to argue that the story of Pocahontas—her love of white men, her self-sacrifice, her marriage and conversion—is deeply embedded in seventeenth-century dramatic accounts of colonialism. The figure of Pocahontas is both threatening and benevolent, and drawing on Bhabha's argument regarding the dialectical and ambivalent sign of the colonized that threatens to disrupt the authority of the colonizer,[67] I demonstrate that her myth needs to be repeatedly restaged because what she represents—sexual chaos and barbarity—can never be absolutely eradicated.

Chapter 1 then turns to Shakespeare's *Tempest* and John Fletcher's *The Sea Voyage*. Chapter 2 follows with later seventeenth-century adaptations of *The Tempest*: John Dryden's and William Davenant's *Tempest*, Thomas Duffet's *The Mock Tempest*, and Thomas Durfey's *A Common-Wealth of Women*. These two chapters link the historical accounts of colonialism to the drama and also bridge the historical gap between the colonial plays of the early seventeenth century and those of the Restoration. I argue that in the seventeenth-century *Tempests* the upper-class courtship narrative of appropriation—based on the European hero seducing and/or marrying the native woman—functions as a means to promote the colonial project and to repress threats of political chaos within English culture. The various redactions of *The Tempest* mirror contemporary perceptions of the relationship between the government and the people as well as between Europe and its colonies during the seventeenth century. In Shakespeare's play, the patriarchal authority embodied by Prospero is more or less absolute, and Caliban is "deservedly" under his control; similarly, the patriarchal figure of authority in Fletcher's *Sea Voyage* is presented as stable, and the European women who turn wild are ultimately domesticated by him. Yet in the redactions of *The Tempest* that were written during the Restoration—Dryden's and Davenant's *Tempest*, Duffet's *Mock Tempest*, and Durfey's *Common-Wealth of Women*—patriarchal authority is presented as no longer absolute, and the European woman who has gone native threatens to overpower the patriarchal figure. The native woman's power is most threatening, then, in the revisions of *The Tempest* that were written when the politics of monarchical authority were most violently destabilized. In the Restoration *Tempests*, the native woman, the absent/present black woman, and the European woman who goes native bear the blame for the chaos within the Englishman and the destabilization of patriarchal and monarchical power.

Chapter 3 examines Dryden's and Howard's *Indian Queen* and Dryden's *Indian Emperour* to argue that, like *The Tempest* and its seventeenth-century redactions, these plays project the politics of colonialism onto the romantic myth of the native woman. To this end, I look closely at the historical figure of Malinche and the woman-as-land metaphor in the context of the Spanish conquest of Mexico. As in the legend of Pocahontas, Malinche's story represses the wildness within the European white man and justifies the necessity for colonization. Both of Dryden's plays depict the Indians as ultimately bringing about their own destruction; the indigenous people therefore require the authority of the conqueror to bring about social, political, and economic progress and religious redemption. The barbarity of the native people is projected onto the figure of the sexually savage indigenous woman and her absolute domination (or eradication) becomes necessary to bring about political and religious stability for both the Indians and the Spaniards.

Chapter 4 analyzes Aphra Behn's colonial discourse in *The Widow Ranter, or The History of Bacon in Virginia*. Behn's play is loosely based on historical accounts of Nathaniel Bacon's rebellion in the Virginia colony in 1675–1676 and the events surrounding the fall of James II in England in the 1680s. In this chapter, I examine late-seventeenth-century politics in England as well as the history of the Bacon rebellion in relation to *The Widow Ranter*, to argue that Behn creates a radical ambivalence in her dramatic alteration of history. Throughout the play, there is a crisis in meaning and categories in the (missing) link between historical "truth" and dramatic fiction in the performances of gender, race, class, and power.

By the 1680s, when Behn wrote *The Widow Ranter*, economic conditions in England may have dictated a more optimistic view of England's colonial future. Behn's play, therefore, functions as a natural ending for my study of seventeenth-century colonial drama. The century commences with great difficulty for English colonists in North America and ends with a promising colonial future, in which penniless English gentlemen solve their economic problems, in part, by marrying white landholding daughters and widows in the New World. Unlike the playwrights before her, then, Behn no longer needs to displace English desires for empire building onto the Spanish or Portuguese. "Thus in the beginning," as Locke writes optimistically in 1682, "all the World was *America*."[68] For Behn's gentlemen characters in *The Widow Ranter*, all the world is *Virginia*.

# ONE

# *The Tempest, The Sea Voyage*, and the Pocahontas Myth

The multiple revisions of Shakespeare's *Tempest* in the seventeenth century demonstrate the cultural desire for a reconciliation of the ambivalent discourse of English colonization in its early phases, as Paul Brown suggests.[1] But perhaps more significantly, these redactions of *The Tempest* suggest also how English political discourse attempts to unravel its own complex ideological contradictions through the fictional encounters of the white man and the other. The New World, as it is recreated and represented on the English stage, functions as a testing ground for resolving the rifts and discontinuities in English politics and culture. The ideological appropriation of the other culture by seventeenth-century authors takes place for self-serving purposes: to establish the difference between a supposedly savage people and a civilized English nation and to reinforce conservative theories of government, such as those of Filmer and James I. In chapters 1 and 2, I will argue that the female body, both native and European, is figured as the image over which the testing of conservative theories of government and the attempted reconciliation of disparate seventeenth-century English ideologies occur.[2] These plays use the conventions of upper-class courtship to attempt to justify the subjection or eradication of the New World Native American population.[3] But the conquest of the native in and by the conventions of the courtly romance mystifies, and hence justifies, the politics of the imperial project.

The differences among *The Tempests* written during the early and those written in the later seventeenth century are great. In Shakespeare's and Fletcher's plays, patriarchal authority, though temporarily destabilized, is restored; yet in the plays that were written during the Restoration, the political authority of the king is no longer absolute or heroically rendered. This difference may result from the vastly different political climates during which these plays were written: Shakespeare and Fletcher wrote before England's civil war, while Dryden, Davenant, Duffet, and Durfey wrote during the Restoration, when the political scene was filled with factionalism and the ideology of absolutism was far less stable.[4] In the Restoration redactions of *The Tempest*, which I examine in chapter 2, patriarchal authority cannot fully restrain the savagery of the New World. It is woman who bears responsibility for the invasion of wildness; native and white women tempt men to become wild, and white women become uncivilized others.[5] Although the other female body is potentially a positive ideal for women, as in John Fletcher's *The Sea Voyage* and Thomas Durfey's *A Common-Wealth of Women*, the Indian woman and the white woman who has gone native are ultimately constructed as dangerous, unruly, and corrupt, and they are scapegoated for the destabilization of European patriarchal authority.

Despite the enormous popularity of *The Tempest* during the late seventeenth century, few contemporary critics have examined the significance of the revisions by John Dryden and William Davenant, Thomas Duffet, and Thomas Durfey. The adaptations of *The Tempest* played frequently throughout the Restoration.[6] The first revision of Shakespeare's *Tempest* was John Fletcher's *The Sea Voyage*, licensed in 1622—the year of the great Indian revolt and massacre in Virginia. Following the Interregnum, Dryden's and Davenant's adaptation, *The Tempest, or The Enchanted Island*, was first performed in November 1667.[7] The operatic version of the *Enchanted Island* appeared in 1674. George Guffey notes that the 1674 operatic version of *Enchanted Island* was "very likely 'the most popular play of the Restoration period.' "[8] It was performed 163 times between 19 November 1674 and 31 January 1746.[9] Apparently the enormous success of the operatic version led Thomas Duffet to write his *Mock-Tempest: or The Enchanted Castle*, which was first performed in 1674. Finally, Thomas Durfey's *A Common-Wealth of Women*, an adaptation of Fletcher's *The Sea Voyage*, was licensed in 1685.

While Shakespeare's *Tempest* has been studied in great depth by new historicists, feminist critics, and Shakespeare scholars, most of the revisions of the play—despite their popularity—have gone practically unnoticed.[10] To what can we attribute this neglect? For one, these plays are complexly engaged in the discourses of colonialism, gender, and race, and I would argue that they necessitate a rethinking of traditional critical assumptions about Restoration literary culture. They demand that we reexamine the relationship of European expansionism to Restoration politics and the effects of colonialism on literary constructions of gender, race, and class in late-seventeenth-century England. This study, therefore, attempts to extend the insights of such works as *The*

*New Eighteenth Century, Cultural Readings of the Restoration, Women, "Race,"
and Writing, Things of Darkness, Ends of Empire*, and *Tropicopolitans*, which
demonstrate the necessity for and benefits of the use of theoretical models in
analyzing literature and culture of the Restoration and eighteenth century.[11]
New critical and theoretical insights not only illuminate these plays, they have
a higher threshold for explaining the complicated political and ideological
contexts of the late seventeenth century. Traditional literary critics, such as
Earl Miner, Maximillian Novak, George Robert Guffey, and Katherine Eisamen
Maus, for example, who provide insightful analyses of Dryden's and Davenant's *Enchanted Island*, suggest that the island provides an ideological space
to examine European models of government and to examine contemporary
political struggles.[12] Yet while their analyses are extremely valuable (and I will
draw upon them in this chapter), they tell a one-sided story. These critics do
not consider how power relations in the *Tempests* are encoded in the female
body—native, African, and European. They focus their attention solely on the
texts' reconstruction of the rifts within patriarchal Restoration politics, such
as the crisis of divine authority and political rebellion, without examining
what is at stake for women and non-Europeans in this discourse. In doing so,
they fail to see the ways in which overlapping constructions of race and
gender are necessary to our understanding of Restoration culture. The identification of woman-as-land, as I discuss in the Introduction, means that these
traditional critics are also downplaying the desire to exploit the resources
(natural and human) of the New World. As Gayatri Spivak argues, it "should
not be possible to read" British literature without "remembering that imperialism, understood as England's social mission, was a crucial part of the cultural
representation of England to the English. The role of literature in the production of cultural representation should not be ignored."[13] I would argue similarly that the study of the representations of gender *and* race in the literature
of the late seventeenth century is crucial to our understanding of English
culture during the Restoration.

Before examining the seventeenth-century *Tempests*, I want to turn to the
myth of Pocahontas, the Native American woman who supposedly enabled
the Virginia colony to succeed. Pocahontas's role in early English colonial history is vastly important: her appropriation functions as a symbol of the potential for the economic success of the English in the New World. Although
she is not directly named in Shakespeare's *Tempest* and its seventeenth-century
revisions, traces of her tale are relevant to the racial and gender discourses of
these plays. I want to suggest that Pocahontas is one of the key figures whose
vexed "surrogation," to borrow Joseph Roach's term (the futile attempt to
replay her in performance), takes place throughout the seventeenth-century

*Tempests*. Indeed, Pocahontas's feared and desired presence penetrates these plays.

Like the woman-as-land metaphor examined in the Introduction, Pocahontas is constituted ambivalently: she is both virgin and whore, Christianized native and untamable other.[14] In effect, the myth of Pocahontas produces and is produced by a dichotomized view of the New World as benevolent and dangerous. Rayna Green calls this dichotomy the "Pocahontas Perplex," suggesting that the figure of the native woman stands both for the "New World's promises and [its] dangers." She is a "Mother-Goddess figure—full-bodied, powerful, nurturing but dangerous—embodying the opulence and peril of the New World."[15]

As the story supposedly goes, Pocahontas, at twelve years old, met John Smith, saved him from her father Powhatan's plan to kill him,[16] brought the colonists much needed food, and warned them about attacks from her tribe, and, in brief, repeatedly saved their lives. After Smith departed from Virginia, she was captured for a ransom and married John Rolfe two years after her abduction. The marriage of John Rolfe and Pocahontas took place on April 5, 1614. At the wedding Pocahontas was baptized Rebecka. She was the "first *Christian* ever of that Nation: The first *Virginian* ever spake *English*, or had a Child in marriage by an *English* Man."[17] Pocahontas's marriage, conversion, and production of future English subjects marks the beginning of the domination of Protestant culture in North America. When Powhatan heard of the intended marriage, he found it, according to Ralph Hamor, a "thing acceptable to him, as he appeared by his sudden consent thereunto." After the wedding, Hamor continues, "ever since we have had friendly commerce and trade, not only with *Powhatan* himselfe, but also with his subjects around us; so as now I see why the Collonie should not thrive a pace."[18] When the Chicohominies, a neighboring tribe, heard of the truce between the colonists and Powhatan, they became "not onely trustie friends, but even King IAMES his subjects and tributaries . . . and . . . they would intreate Sir Thomas *Dale* as King IAMES his deputie to be their supreme head, king and governor."[19] The marriage of Pocahontas and Rolfe supposedly led the Chicohominies to become dutiful and compliant subjects who "chose rather to subject themselves to us [the colonists], then being enemies to both, to expose & lay themselves open to Powhatans tiranny & oppression."[20] Notably, Reverand Whitakers, Thomas Dale, and Rolfe all cover up the adultery committed through the interracial union: there is no mention of what happened to Pocahontas's first husband, Kocoum, in their accounts of the marriage.[21] Pocahontas, as Strachey writes, was "now marryed to a pryvate Captayne called Kocoum some 2. years synce"[22] before her abduction and subsequent marriage to Rolfe. Pocahontas' prior marriage to a Native American man has been repressed in later historical texts as well.[23]

The romance narrative of the Indian princess' story disguises the real politics of the Pocahontas-Rolfe marriage: the establishment of peace—a precondition for economic prosperity because the English were still outnumbered—led to the growth of tobacco agriculture, the colony's first profitable commodity. Significantly, it was John Rolfe who first "succeeded in growing tobacco in Virginia that could rival Spanish exports," and tobacco "finally solved the colony's problem for paying for supplies."[24] William Warren Jenkins explains, "If John Smith was the political and tactical savior of the Jamestown settlement, John Rolfe played a scarcely less vital role in securing the colony's existence. It was he who gave the first real life to the settlement's economy."[25] In the Pocahontas myth, then, the conquering of the native woman enables both Smith and Rolfe to empower English traders, merchants, and investors through economic growth in the New World.

According to Young, Dale brought Pocahontas-Rebecka and Rolfe, and their son Thomas, to England in 1616, "to publicize the success of Jamestown."[26] As the first Indian from Virginia to become a Christian, Pocahontas symbolized the success of the colonial project, and, as a result, she was honored and feted by the English. As a princess, she was treated, at least in part, with the attention of a royal, as the English imposed their own sense of political and social hierarchies upon the Native Americans. Peter Hulme argues, "Pocahontas . . . can in the end assume an ideologically potent mythic status despite her race only because she is an intelligent, pure and, above all, *noble* Indian."[27] By marking and emphasizing her "superior" class status, the English attempted to set her apart from other Indians, to deflect fears of miscegenation, and to deflect fears about the status of her hybrid heirs from the Rolfe union.[28]

I would argue, however, that Indian nobility in the Pocahontas myth functions simultaneously as a mockery, a form of play, a persistent reminder of the impossibility of reinventing the Native American as truly royal or English. When Pocahontas's father-chief was crowned king (at James I's command), for example, as a measure to subdue and win the friendship of Powhatan, Smith viewed the idea as "grotesque"[29] (and he berated James I for it in his description of the event); yet an elaborate ceremony—including the gift of a bed furnished in typical fashion for English royalty—was performed nevertheless. This incident establishes the contradictory and paradoxical nature of English spectacular conceptions and presentations of Native Americans as regal. Although Powhatan is distinguished from other Indians who were *not noble*, in Smith's accounts, he could never be fully monarchical according to English standards.

Pocahontas's royal performance in England also functions in an ambivalent, conflicted, and contradictory manner. Set apart from other Indians, she must always remind the English that she is the 'rare' specimen, the only one of her kind to marry and unify the English and Indian nations. Pocahontas's special status repeatedly begs the uneasy and unresolved question: but what of other nonroyal Indians? Can they, should they, be subdued, saved, married, bred with? Pocahontas is always different (different from whites and other nonroyal Indians as well), always not quite the "Lady." In a letter to Queen Ann (discussed in depth below), Smith suggests that, if Pocahontas is not well received on this visit, she may become wild and vicious and turn her scorn on the English people. Pocahontas may have self-consciously adopted her role as an English noblewoman, like the Mohawk kings Joseph Roach describes in *Cities of the Dead*, but her conflicted surrogation, like theirs, belies the complex interconnections of the English and their colonial relations, the feared "specter of generations threatening to be born" and invade the English and their homeland.[30]

After Pocahontas's successful conversion, the colonists in Virginia attempted (unsuccessfully) to subdue the Chesapeake people by forcing them to convert. After Pocahontas's death in 1617, and Powhatan's death in 1618, however, tension between the colonists and the Native Americans rapidly mounted. In 1622, Native Americans attacked the colony, killing one third of the population. As a result of the massacre, the white colonists' attitude toward the Native Americans became overtly and radically hostile and continued to be so throughout the rest of the century. John Smith writes that, "some will say [the massacre] will be good for the Plantation, because now we have just cause to destroy [the Indians] by all meanes possible." While he also suggests that it might have been easier to "civilize" the Native Americans in a less aggressive manner, he ultimately concludes that using violence is preferable and more expedient: "Rome grew by oppression, and rose upon the backe of her enemies: and the Spaniards have had many of those counterbuffes, more than we. Columbus, upon his returne the West-Indies into Spaine, having left his people with the Indies, in peace and promise of good usage . . . [,] at his returne back found not one of them living, but all treacherously slaine by the Salvages."[31] Smith thus determines that force against the Indians of Virginia is not only heroic—"Rome grew by oppression"—but necessary to the colony's survival. The method by which Pocahontas is "civilized," then, remains an idealized and romanticized means of subjugating the indigenous people of Virginia.

Inherent in the deep-seated ambivalence about the Native American woman's nature in the Pocahontas tale is the fear of the white male's going native. Historical accounts demonstrate that many white settlers abandoned the colony to live with natives, "where," as Hulme writes, "at least before 1622, they were rapidly and unproblematically assimilated.[32] Seventeenth-century historical accounts by Smith and other settlers reinforce the view that throughout the century, without strict political rule, the colony would have been destroyed or at least split into factions. Within the Virginia settlement, there were many internal disputes, and the colony was close to self-destruction on numerous occasions. During the first six months of the founding of the Virginia Settlement, all but thirty-eight of the first settlers died. The initial settlers were ill-equipped to deal with the wilderness; the gentry refused to work, and the artisans who were sent with them were not prepared to produce food. Political battles ensued over the establishing of a council. Smith, who served as the colony's leader until 1609, when gunpowder wounds forced him to return to England, complained that many early settlers refused to work for their food. As a result, only a small number survived. As Smith writes, the English who did not find gold or silver, "had little or no care of any thing, but to pamper their bellies, to fly away with our Pinnaces, or procure their meanes to returne for England."[33] After 1610, as Warren M. Billings states, the colony was held together only through strict governmental rule and a "series of regulations that subjected the colonists to martial law and discipline."[34]

Perhaps the most striking example of the English man's going wild in Virginia occurred during the period known as "starving time," in the fall of 1609 through the winter of 1610, after Smith's departure for England and before the arrival of the Deputy Governor Thomas Gates, who was shipwrecked and temporarily detained in Bermuda.[35] After Smith's departure, Pocahontas stopped assisting the colonists with the delivery of much needed food and warnings about attacks from the Native Americans. An eyewitness observed that:

> so great was our famine, that a Salvage we slew and buried, the poorer sort tooke him up againe and eat him; and so did divers one another boyled and stewed with roots and herbs: And one amongst the rest did kill his wife, powdered her, and had eaten part of her before it was knowne; for which hee was executed, as hee well deserved: now whether shee was better roasted, boyled or carbonado'd, I know not; but of such a dish as powdered wife I never heard of . . .
>
> That was the time, which still to this day we called the starving time; it were too vile to say, and scarce to be beleeved, what we endured.[36]

Another witness of starving time writes:

> Men did crazy things which seem incredible, as to dig up corpses out of graves and eat them—and some have licked up blood which hath fallen from their weak fellows. And amongst the rest, this was most lamentable, that one of the colony murdered his wife, ripped the child out of her womb and threw

it in the river, and after chopped the mother in pieces and salted her for his food, the same not being discovered before he had eaten part thereof.[37]

During starving time the English man becomes all that he fears most about the natives. Notably, in the first passage, the "poorer sort" bear the brunt of barbarity. In an oddly mirrored effect, the anarchy within the colony is figured by the horror of a white man eating a woman—the inverse of the colonists' fear of being devoured by a native woman. English savagery is depicted, also, as the destruction of the traditional heterosexual family, as a husband rips the child from his wife's womb and devours her body. Woman, therefore, bears the pain of the Englishman's wildness and the future of English civility is symbolically destroyed by this violent act: the death of the child and the woman occur at the same time. As a result of the chaos in the Virginia colony, the London Company determined that the only means for the colony's survival was strict governmental rule. Virginia's governor was therefore made absolute ruler, and for six years following starving time the colony's "survival was the direct result of the stern government."[38] The reassertion of a patriarchal authority—which mirrors monarchical authority and James I's authoritarian rule—was crucial to the repression of wildness within and the colonizing of the wilderness without.

In seventeenth-century historical texts, English male fears about going native are deflected onto significant but ambivalently portrayed aspects of the Pocahontas tale. In Smith's letter to Queen Anne in 1616—written as an introduction to Pocahontas on the eve of her visit to England, and after Pocahontas's conversion to Christianity and marriage to Rolfe—he praises Pocahontas for her repeated benevolent acts on behalf of the colonists, despite her father's wishes:

[r]elief . . . was commonly brought us by this Lady *Pocahontas*, notwithstanding all these Passages, when unconstant Fortune turn'd our Peace to War, this tender Virgin would still not spare to dare to visit us; and by her our Jars have been oft appeased, and our Wants still supplied. . . . [S]he, next under God, was still the Instrument to preserve this Colony from Death, Famine, and utter Confusion, which if, in those Times, had once been dissolv'ed, *Virginia* might have lain, as it was at our first Arrival, till this Day.[39]

In this description, Pocahontas is presented as a nurturing and virginal savior. However, at the end of Smith's letter to Queen Anne, Smith hints at an alternative side to Pocahontas; he warns that if Pocahontas is not well received upon her visit to England with Rolfe, "her present Love to us, and Christianity, might turn to such Scorn and Fury, as to divert all this Good to the worst of

Evil."[40] Pocahontas is thus endowed with the power to preserve or decimate the colony. Without proper treatment, Pocahontas may return to what seems to be an innate barbarism and destroy the fledgling colony.

More importantly perhaps, the Indian woman's dangerous side is displayed most overtly in her sexuality. Smith's description of what he calls *The Virginia Mask* (1608), which was performed for his benefit by a group of Native American women, demonstrates his fear of being sexually overpowered by the promiscuous woman:[41]

In a fayre plaine field they made a fire, before which, he [Smith] sitting upon a mat, suddainly amongst the woods was heard such a hydeous noise and shreeking, that the English betooke themselves to their armes, and seized on two or three old men by them, supposing Powhatan with all his power was come to surprise them. But presently Pocahontas came, willing him [Smith] to kill her if any hurt were intended. . . . Then presently they were presented with this anticke; thirtie young women came naked out of the woods, onely covered behind and before with a few greene leaves, their bodies all painted, some of one colour, some of another, but all differing, their leader had a fayre payre of Bucks hornes on her head, and an Otters skinne at her girdle, and another at her arme, a quiver of arrowes at her backe, a bow and arrowes in her hand; the next had in her hand a sword, another a club, another a pot-sticke; all horned alike. . . . These fiends with most hellish shouts and cryes, rushing from among the trees, cast themselves in a ring about the fire, singing and dauncing with most excellent ill varietie oft falling into their infernall passions, and solemnly againe to sing and daunce; having spent near an houre in this Mascarado, as they entred in like manner they departed. . . . [T]hey solemnly invited him [Smith] to their lodgings, where he was no sooner within the house, but all these Nymphes more tormented him then ever, with crowding, pressing, and hanging about him, most tediously crying, Love you not me? love you not me?[42]

*The Virginia Mask* demonstrates that the female natives function as a spectacle of the dangers of the New World for the white male English audience: these are wild and infernal warrior seductresses. Pocahontas and the native women perform as the object of the male gaze.[43] Yet, as this passage also demonstrates, the women's performance dangerously reverses the position of the white male observer—he becomes the object of the native female desire. Smith is pursued by the performers, and he fears being overwhelmed or corrupted by them. As Robert J. C. Young argues, the discourse of racial hybridity "circulate[s] around an ambivalent axis of desire and aversion."[44] This desire to possess the native woman and keep her at a distance is replayed throughout the seventeenth century precisely because it is circular and unresolvable. The

English long to possess the New World, yet they fear the changes in their own culture and the threat to their own identity that this possession must necessarily bring.

The desire for and fear of Pocahontas's sexuality in Smith's response to *The Virginia Mask* is evidenced also in Rolfe's concern about marrying Pocahontas. With Rolfe, however, the myth of Pocahontas succeeds in rupturing the distance between observer and observed and racial distinctions are not maintained. Rolfe's marriage to the native woman is, ostensibly, part of the overall missionary project of the colony to Christianize the Indians. Many early English colonists believed the "way to *tame* the savages was to bring them into the Anglican faith."[45] In the first twelve months after Pocahontas had been taken captive by the colonists, Sir Thomas Dale asked Alexander Whitakers, a missionary and minister, to instruct her in Christianity.[46] Dale explains that Pocahontas was *"carefully instructed in the Christian Religion[,] . . . renounced publickly her countrey Idolatry, openly confessed her Christian faith, was, as she desired, baptised, and is since married to an English Gentleman of good standing."*[47] For Dale, peace was ensured by the marriage, and the union could be sanctified because Pocahontas relinquished her cultural identity and converted to Christianity. The purpose of the union of Rolfe and Pocahontas was both the saving of one soul and the preservation of the colony. Thus, for Dale, salvation is described in religious *and* economic terms. Whitakers also viewed the marriage as significant for religious reasons. He writes that Pocahontas was *"married to an honest and discreete English Gentleman* Master Rolfe, and that after she had openly renounced her countrey idolatry, confessed the faith of Jesus Christ, and was baptised; which thing Sir Thomas Dale had laboured a long time to ground in her."[48] For Whitaker, the marriage is blessed by Pocahontas's religious conversion, but his description implies that the conversion was forced—Christianity was "ground into her." Both Whitaker and Dale are overtly concerned with masking the sexual aspects of the marriage—there is no mention of passion or love in their descriptions. Instead, they emphasize the extraordinary religious and cultural control over the Native American that is achieved.

Rolfe also portrays his marriage to Pocahontas as a means of bringing a savage to Christ. In his letter to Dale, requesting that he be allowed to marry Pocahontas, he writes,

Let therefore this my . . . protestation, which here I make between god and my own conscience, be a sufficient witness, at the dreadfull day of iugdement . . . to condemn me herein, if my chiefest intent and purpose be not, to strive with all my power of body and minde, in the undertaking of so mightie a matter, no way led (so farre forth as many weaknesse may permit) with the unbridled desire of carnell affection: but for the good of this plantation for the honour of our countrie, for the glory of God, for my own salvation, and for the converting to the true knowledge of God and Iesus Christ, and unbeleeving creature, namely Pokahuntas. To whom my hartie and best thoughts are, and have a long time bin so intangled, and inthralled in so intricate a laborinth, that I was even awearied to unwinde myselfe thereout. But almighty God, who never faileth his, that truely invoke his holy name, hath opened the gate and led me by the hand.[49]

As in Whitaker's and Dale's letters, Rolfe's anxiety about the white man's carnal desire for the native woman and, hence, the potential for the white man to go native and jeopardize his racial and national purity, are concealed by the supposed religious and economic advantages of the union. Rolfe justifies his marriage to Pocahontas by stating that it is for the good of his soul as well as hers. But his letter also reveals his sexual desire for Pocahontas; he admits to feeling trapped, overpowered, and exhausted—language which suggests sexual activity, albeit in anxious terms. His discourse of repressing his own sexual desires in order to act on behalf of the colony and of God is restaged throughout the seventeenth century. Each colonizer's soul is at stake when Rolfe enters the colonial project of saving the savage; by converting the Native American woman, he demonstrates his own moral worth and the moral worth of the colony. Pocahontas's religious conversion acts to bless and sanctify the economic rationale for colonization.

The Rolfe-Pocahontas union was not repeated as a means of colonization in English North American colonies. Because intermarriage with the Indians was considered (for the most part) an aberration in the seventeenth century, Pocahontas's tale functioned as a nostalgic and archetypal example of what could have been. After 1622, as I discussed in the Introduction, increasing legal attempts were made to keep white colonists from marrying and/or fornicating with Native Americans and people of African descent in Virginia. In 1705, following his account of Pocahontas's marriage to Rolfe, Robert Beverley writes:

[i]ntermarriage had been indeed the Method proposed very often by the *Indians* in the Beginning, urging it frequently as a certain Rule, that the *English* were not their Friends, if they refused it. And I cant but think it wou'd have been happy for that Country, had they embraced this Proposal. . . . [M]any, if not most, of the *Indians* would have been converted to Christianity by this kind Method; the Country would have been full of People, by the Preservation of the many *Christians* and *Indians* that fell in the Wars between them. Besides, there would have been a Continuance of all those Nations of *Indians* that are now dwindled away to nothing by their frequent Removals, or are

fled to other Parts; not to mention the Invitation that so much Success and Prosperity would have been for others to have gone over and settled there, instead of the Frights and Terrors that were produced by all those Misfortunes that happen'd.[50]

Beverley suggests that had the practice of intermarriage continued, the Indians would have been saved, and the colonists would have prospered. The benefits are described in both spiritual and economic terms. For Beverley, then, the marriage of Pocahontas and Rolfe was a symbol of the perfect union of the white man and the native: economically it was beneficial for both. As discussed earlier, for those who idealized interracial unions as a means of civilizing the other and conquering the New World, it was Pocahontas's royal lineage which distinguished her from ordinary "savages" and thus added to her appeal as an ideal mate for the English colonist. The implication is that intermarriage reinforces class-based assumptions that lead the English to project onto the Indian political structures the characteristics of Nations possessing the hierarchies and values similar to those of the Europeans.

The Pocahontas myth presents colonization in ways that are overdetermined in the drama throughout the seventeenth century: Native Americans are feared and desired, but ultimately must be subjugated, exploited, and evacuated from coveted land. Although native people might be assimilated into English culture, they may never be trusted. Native women are sexually wild and uncontrollable, and contact with them and their people may turn the English men and women wild as well. The final determination that Smith proposes and that the Virginia and other North American English colonists followed is that interracial assimilation is a nice sentimental idea, but it is not a viable means for colonization; extermination is a better, safer, more economical bet. The Pocahontas myth, moreover, crucially intertwines discourses of gender, race, and early Stuart systems of patriarchy, in which kings are posited as "father[s] of the nation." (Although after the deaths of James I and Charles I the "king-as-father of the nation" equation functions in a far more contradictory and vexed fashion, it is always marked by internal divisions and tensions, as later chapters in this work will show.)[51] Pocahontas and the native peoples she represents are figured as unruly men and women who need and want to be dominated by a patriarchal father figure. In this way, Pocahontas paves the way for a morally justifiable destruction of Native Americans and the appropriation of their land. This sentimentalized and romanticized version of colonization, however, never ceases to raise anxiety, fear, and aversion, hence it needs to be replayed in the supposedly safe, contained world of the English stage—far away from "real" Native Americans and the "real" colony in the New World.

Shakespeare's *Tempest* stages and mediates the problems of the legitimacy of royal authority through the female other.[52] Prospero has taken control of the island which originally belonged to the powerful "foul witch Sycorax" (I.ii.258), the "hag" who was "so strong/ That [she] could controul the moon" (60).[53] Not only has Prospero claimed ownership over Sycorax's former land as well as her son, but he has done so by appropriating the other female's magical powers; he has studied books that allow him to master nature—and this mastery in the seventeenth century has gendered implications. Hulme points out how Prospero's power is "supernatural" only on the island: his "magic is at his disposal on the island but not off of it." Prospero's "magic" is linked, historically, to accounts of early explorer's and early colonist's use of "technology" as a means to subdue and conquer non-Europeans; more importantly, it is linked, as well, to how Europeans defined supposedly less civilized nations as lesser than themselves.[54] Michael Adas argues, "technological achievement did much to determine the extent to which its people were esteemed or held in contempt. It also had considerable bearing on the levels allotted to different peoples in the hypothetical hierarchies of human development which were beginning to form in the European imagination."[55] Not surprisingly, then, Prospero's "superiority" is depicted as moral as well as mystical; his books bleach the blackness and evil of Sycorax's magic. Symbolic of Prospero's power is his control over Sycorax's former spirit Ariel, and it is through Ariel that Prospero's dukedom is restored. When Ariel asks for his "freedom," Prospero chides the spirit and reminds him of how he saved him from Sycorax:

> Thou, my slave,
> As thou report'st thyself, wast . . . [Sycorax's] servant.
> And, for thou wast a spirit too delicate
> To act her earthy and abhorred commands,
> Refusing her grand hests, she did confine thee,
> By help of her more potent ministers,
> And in her most unmitigable rage,
> into a cloven pine; within which rift
> Imprisoned thou didst painfully remain
> A dozen years.
>
> (I.ii.270–279)

Prospero controls Sycorax's former servant, and he justifies this treatment by claiming that he actually saved Ariel; moreover, Prospero suggests that he could save Ariel only because he is more powerful than Sycorax. Caliban similarly recognizes that Prospero is more powerful than Sycorax and the non-European magical tradition she represents: "I must obey [Prospero], His art is of such pow'r/It would control my dam's god, Setebos,/And make a vassal of him" (I.ii.373–375). Within the context of colonialist discourse and English politics in the early seventeenth century, Prospero's "magic" mystifies the colonial project; it legitimates his control of nature and non-European peoples. Caliban is awed by Prospero's power, and Ariel is made to feel beholden to the former Duke.

Although Sycorax is no longer alive, she is ever-present in Prospero's mind. She is the shadow which follows Prospero, and, as Orgel suggests, she "embodies to an extreme degree all the negative assumptions about women that he and Miranda have exchanged."[56] Sycorax is sexually wild—she is pregnant and without a husband; she serves as a symbol of the native woman who is dangerous and/or sexually uncontrollable.[57] She represents everything his virginal daughter must not become, and it is Prospero's duty as a European father to ensure that Miranda remains chaste. His control of the island derives from the patrilineal values that he brings with him from Europe; thus Prospero's role as "ruler" is discursively and ideologically linked to his fatherly authority over his daughter. Shakespeare's *Tempest*, like most plays during this period, presents the father's control of the female body—European and non-European—as the means through which European patriarchal authority is maintained. In order to restore his royal power, Prospero must control Miranda to ensure that she marries a European nobleman; she is therefore kept separate from the son of Sycorax, Caliban.[58] By appropriating and repressing the role of the woman, mother, and other in the play, Prospero manages to regain his throne and bring about a reconciliation of political division among the islanders and among the Europeans he shipwrecks there.[59]

Prospero feels justified in his treatment of Caliban because, according to the former Duke, Caliban attempted to rape Miranda. Caliban's version of the European colonization of the island differs greatly from Prospero's, however. According to Caliban, Prospero has stolen and thus symbolically raped Caliban's property.

> This island's mine by Sycorax my mother,
> Which thou tak'st from me, When thou 'cam'st first,
> Thou stroks't me, and made much of me; would'st give me
> Water with berries in't; and teach me how
> To name the bigger light, and how the less,
> That burn by day and night. And then I love'd thee
> And show'd thee all the qualities o'th' isle,
> The fresh springs, brine pits, barren place and fertile.

Cursed be I that I did so! All the charms
Of Sycorax—toads, beetles, bats, light on you!
For I am all the subjects that you have,
Which first was mine own king; and here you sty me
In this hard rock, whiles you do keep from me
The rest 'o 'th island.

(I.ii.331–345)

Caliban's speech draws on the contemporary history of Virginia.[60] In North America the Indians were generally hospitable to the Europeans until they found their land "encroached upon, their forests cleared, their game driven off" at which point they "retaliated."[61] The colonizers paradoxically interpreted the Indians' retaliation as treacherous; they believed that the Indians could not be trusted, that behind their mask of friendliness lurked violence.[62] As Caliban says, initially Prospero 'made much of him,' inducing him to show Prospero how to survive on the island. But then Prospero imprisons Caliban in a rock, keeps him as a slave, and justifies this treatment by calling him a lazy, ungrateful, and sexually lascivious barbarian. Caliban indeed fits seventeenth-century English stereotypes of nonwhite males as sexual threats to white women. Kathleen M. Brown argues that the strong bias against interracial unions between black, mixed race, or Indian men with white women in Virginia led to "the sexualization of race."[63] Indeed, Caliban's role as sexual threat to Miranda is overdetermined—it is Prospero's and Shakespeare's justification for the oppression of the other in the name of Christian decency and sexual morality.

Significantly, Caliban's character draws uneasily on ambiguous stereotypes of distinct non-European cultural groups. Caliban is the son of the African Sycorax, but as pointed out in the above paragraph, he also functions symbolically as a native Indian of the island.[64] Caliban's slippage of identity thus points to a radical ambivalence in the colonial drama of *The Tempest*. Caliban performs as an overt theatrical hybridization of different cultures—in other words, his imprecise rendering marks him as fictional; yet he also performs as a fearful reminder of the dangers of miscegenation and the blurring of races. By making him African, Shakespeare avoids, in part, dealing with the origins of ownership of the land, and the island is thus justifiably available for white Europeans, and the ghosts of absent Indians function only in ways that are useful to Prospero. However, Caliban's imprecise surrogation also points to English anxieties about interracial contact and the impossibility of dominating the other in the drama. Neither the native Indian nor the African can be fully controlled or erased through this ambiguous and ambivalent rendering of the non-European.

Although Caliban is held to be a monster by Prospero, he is also necessary to his European master. Like the European colonists who needed the natives for their survival, Prospero tells Miranda that while Caliban is a "poisonous slave [and] devil" (I.ii.318), they nevertheless "cannot miss him. He does make our fire,/Fetch in our wood, and serves in offices/ That profit us" (I.ii.311–313). Indeed, Prospero's status as "master" is based on his having servants who perform physical labor. As Stephen Greenblatt suggests, this is a re-creation of the gentlemanly or noble authority in the New World; labor distinguishes Prospero from the lower classes and Indians.[65] In act 3, Ferdinand's degrading punishment is to carry logs, which signifies Prospero's power over him. Ironically, even Gonzalo's supposedly egalitarian vision of a common-wealth in act 2 evokes the presence of a nonwhite subject who serves the European. Gonzalo states that if he were king of a colony, there would be

> No use of metal, corn, or wine, or oil;
> No occupation; all men idle, all;
> And women too, but innocent and pure;
> No sovereignty . . .
> All things in common nature should produce
> Without sweat or endeavor. Treason, felony,
> Sword, pike, knife, gun, or need of any engine
> Would I not have; but nature should bring forth,
> Of it own kind, all foison, all abundance,
> To feed my innocent people.
>
> (II.i.158–161;163–169)

In Gonzalo's utopian fantasy, nature's "abundance" obviates the need to labor, as "nature" brings forth enough for everyone. Yet Shakespeare's contemporary audience would know that if all of Gonzalo's "innocent people" (II.i.169) did not "sweat or endeavor," they would not survive. Thus Gonzalo's vision implicitly includes others—native or African slaves—who serve his common-wealth.

In response to Caliban's claims of mistreatment, Prospero argues that his version of their encounter is a lie. Caliban, he claims, was raised on equal footing with his own daughter, "till [Caliban] didst seek to violate/ The honor of my child" (I.ii.347–348). For Prospero, then, the justification for Caliban's servitude hinges on the threat of violation of Miranda's virginity, which is ideologically crucial to both royal honor and colonial exploitation in the play. As a royal European virgin, Miranda serves as the vehicle through which Prospero reasserts his power in Europe, the means to reconcile the rival claim-ants to the Dukedom. The marriage of Ferdinand and Miranda thus serves a double purpose: it both strengthens royal authority and symbolizes the successful and morally justifiable union of the Old World and the New. The European prince marries and colonizes at one and the same time, and this marriage is beneficial to both worlds.

Divine authority, therefore, is restored by the interlocking discourses of the English courtship narrative and the woman-as-land metaphor in the colonial economy. Just as Pocahontas's willing conversion to Christianity and marriage to John Rolfe participates in the discourse of the feminized land of the New World, which is portrayed as an innocent and submissive bride, so too Miranda's desire for Ferdinand (as opposed to Caliban) justifies the European settlement of the New World. If Caliban had had sex with Miranda, they might indeed have "peopled else/This isle with Calibans" (I.ii.350–351). As the early colonizers of the New World well knew, a "peopled" island can be less easily and justifiably appropriated than an uninhabited one. Miranda's virginity, therefore, functions as both a symbol of the bountiful, chaste New World that willingly brings material wealth to its white male conquerors and as the vehicle through which royal power is legitimized in a patrilineal European society.

*The Tempest*, however, points to the crisis in representing race and gender in the drama. English politics are deflected onto other European cultures, distanced from home, and then further displaced onto a blank island. There are no visible black or Native American women in the play. Interracial unions take place elsewhere—Claribel is left in Africa, and the attempted rape of Miranda by Caliban occurs prior to the play's action. Even Miranda's mother is past tense. Perhaps most importantly, native women and their people are performed by stand-ins who do not fit, who remind us of a perverse absence or death. There is no mention of the Indians who were probably on the island before Sycorax, although Caliban reminds us of them at times; instead the island is figured as an empty land which was ruled by a black female imposter and her son. Sycorax and Caliban stand in for the absent Native Americans; they are described throughout the play as the "original" proprietors, yet this always and already rings false. We know that Sycorax comes from elsewhere, and although Caliban may have been born on the island, his familial ties are not native to this place. Miranda as the virginal noblewoman also stands in for the Native American woman; yet this too rings false, because we know she is of European blood. The New World that Shakespeare stages as empty of Native Americans, therefore, can never be fully or stably signified. The performance of the New World must always be riddled with fracture and slippage in *The Tempest*—haunted by the memory or knowledge of Indians who are not represented in the play and by the specters of black women (future slaves?) who cannot be seen.

Fletcher's *The Sea Voyage* (1622) also begins with a family shipwrecked on a deserted island in the New World, a tempest, and female characters who need to be reintegrated into the patriarchal structure. Prior to the beginning of the play, a noble Portuguese family living on "their Plantations in the *Happy Islands*" in the New World has been attacked by French pirates (V.i.135).[66] In trying to escape from these pirates, the family went to sea and the men and women were divided in a storm; the groups landed on different sides of an uninhabited island where they lived without any knowledge of the others' whereabouts for years. The island is divided by a treacherous river which neither group has attempted to cross. The female members of the family— Rosellia, her daughter Clarinda, and her female servants—reside on the fertile side of the island; the males, Sebastian, Rosellia's husband and the father of her daughter Clarinda, and Nicusa, his nephew, live where the land is barren. In the fight with the pirates years before, the male members of the family managed to keep the family's jewels. In the absence of fertile land, the jewels symbolize, in part, the continuity of patrilineal authority, but they also represent capital that cannot be put to productive use on the island. The men need to acquire the fertile side of the island in order to produce material wealth in the New World. They also need to reunite with the women so that the inheritance of this wealth can be secured for a new generation of nobility.

As the play begins, it is many years after the family escaped the French pirates. A tempest rages, and Albert, the son of a leader of the French pirates, and his crew land on the barren side of the island. Like Prospero, Albert arrives with a young virgin whom he must protect, Aminta, sister of Raymond; both are children of the former rival leader of the French pirates. Indeed, the reason for their voyage—and present "miseries," as the sailors state—is Albert's desire to find Aminta's brother, gain his forgiveness for having abducted her, and get his approval to marry her (III.i.104). Albert came into "possession" of Aminta because of a dispute years before between their fathers. When the Portuguese family managed to escape, the Frenchmen blamed each other and became bitter enemies, and "Thence grew *Amintas* rape" (V.i.155). Though the fathers are no longer alive, their sons are still enemies, and the abduction of Aminta is symbolic of their factionalism, as well as the division of the Portuguese family and their exile on the wild island.

In *The Sea Voyage*, the destruction of the patriarchal family and the destabilization of monarchical authority are figured, as well, through bodies of European women who have gone native. On the fertile side of the island, Rosellia has founded what she calls a female commonwealth, in "this blest place,/Inhabited heretofore by warlike women." Rosellia and her women take on the characteristics of the former non-European inhabitants; as Rosellia states, "By their [the former inhabitants'] example" we have taken "execrable oaths never to look/On man, but as a Monster" (II.i.331–332,334,336–337). Rosellia's commonwealth may be based on the following descriptions, from Columbus's and Sir Walter Raleigh's voyages of native women who live independently from men. Even if Fletcher does not borrow directly from Columbus and Raleigh, his Amazons are part of the same cultural heritage that produces an ideological ambivalence about conquest. Columbus writes of an "island" called "Matinino [which] was entirely populated by women, on whom the [male] Caribs descended at certain seasons of the year; and if these women bore sons they were entrusted to the fathers to bring them up." The Indian women kept their daughters.[67] Similarly, Raleigh describes Amazon women in Guiana who, "do accompanie with men but once in a yeere, and for the time of one moneth. . . . If they conceive, and be delivered of a sonne, they returne him to the father, if of a daughter they nourish it, and reteine it. . . . [T]hey are said to be very cruell and bloodthirsty. . . . [T]hey have likewise great store of . . . plates of golde."[68] Columbus also describes another tribe of powerful, independent Indian women who resemble Rosellia and her female commonwealth.

> These women have their legs swathed in cotton cloth from their calf to the knees in order to make them seem stout; they call this practice *coiro* and consider it extremely beautiful. They bind these cloths on so tightly that if one of them happens to get loose this part of the leg is seen to be very thin. . . . These women are extremely fat, some of them being two yards or more round, though well proportioned in other ways. As soon as their children are able to stand and walk they put a bow in their hands and teach them to shoot. They all wear their hair long and loose on their shoulders, and cover no part of their bodies. The lady or female *cacique* whom [the Spaniards] captured said that the whole island was inhabited by women and that the people who had prevented their boats from landing were women also, though there were four men with them who had landed by chance from another island. For a certain period in the year men come from other places to lie with them. The same practice is followed by the women of another island called Martinino, from which arose the story of the Amazons, which the Admiral [Columbus] believed when he saw these women and their strength and courage. They are said to be more intelligent than the women of the other islands.[69]

The Cacique woman is depicted ambivalently by Columbus: she is extraordinarily large and fat, yet "well proportioned in other ways," admirably strong and yet physically dangerous, "intelligent" and yet wild. The real threat to male power in these passages is not the Amazons' unusual physical strength and potential "cruellty," but their overt disinterest in and independence from men. But, this threat also rests on an axis of desire in Columbus. As Greenblatt argues, Columbus's journal is filled with "a sense of the marvelous" which is "associated with longing . . . precisely for what you do not have."[70] It is the native women's self-reliance that clearly intrigues Columbus, as well as the impossibility of locating her *land*. Although he never discovers the home of the independent indigenous women, he captures and takes the "woman cacique and her daughter" from the Canaries to Castile. Supposedly, the Indian woman gives up her rebellion and goes "willingly" with the admiral.

Like the Indian women whom Columbus and Raleigh describe, Fletcher's Amazons are self-sufficient and live independently from men. The Amazons hunt, eat well, and live with ease in the natural world. They appear to the Frenchmen as "Fairies," "Angels" (III.i.255,258), "Nymphs," and "Goddesses" (II.i.200,198); they have been empowered by their roles as Indians. Rosellia repeatedly tells her women how they are no longer "slaves" to men and they thus live in "liberty" (II.i.357,328). The Amazonian commonwealth thus demonstrates that women can function well without male protectors. Indeed, in many instances, they are more powerful than men—while the cowardly Sebastian and Nicusa flee from the French pirates on two occasions, in act Three, scene One, for example, Rosellia and her women warriors disarm the pirates and take them into slavery.

As Diane Dugaw suggests, the figure of the Warrior Woman "highlights . . . the extent to which gender markers are actually customary and external—a social construction." The warrior woman exposes gender as a form of "play."[71] Rosellia's commonwealth thus demonstrates that women "conferr on our selves, and love those fetters/ We fasten to our freedomes" (II.i.326–327). Their subjection to men, in effect, is not natural or absolute—it is something 'put on' like a costume. Yet while the role of the Amazon is positive for the Portuguese women in *The Sea Voyage*, it is also a part they have been compelled to adopt because of their separation from Sebastian and Nicusa. It is only Rosellia who contentedly plays the native woman and relinquishes her heterosexual desire. In this sense, Fletcher implies that freedom and self-sufficiency are not positive goals for women but an uncivilized state that these women adopt by necessity.

Fletcher suggests further that Rosellia's resolution that the young Amazon women never mate with men dooms them to a self-defeating sterility. As the young women claim when confronted with their first sight of a man, if they do not mate with men, their race will die out and "in a few years/The whole World would be peopled/ Onely with Beasts" (II.i.345–346). Indeed, the sexual desire of the young Amazons leads them to rebel against their female leader and thereby threaten the political hierarchy and safety of their commonwealth. When the young female Amazons see Albert, the first man they have encountered on the island, they cannot attack him as they have been taught. Hippolita, one of Clarinda's maids, says, "By my life I cannot hurt him." Crocale, another Amazon says, "Though I lose my head for it, nor I./ I must pitty him, and will" (II.i.216–218). When Clarinda, Rosellia's daughter and their superior, inspects the injured man, she gives up her resolution to kill him. She resolves that they should try to save Albert after his dangerous swim across the treacherous river to seek food. Clarinda commands Hippolita and Crocale to

> Bend his body softly; rub his temples;
> Nay, that shall be my office: how the red
> Steales into his pale lips! . . . fetch the simples
> With which my Mother heal'd my arme
> When last I was wounded by the Bore . . .
> Now he breathes;
> The ayr passing through the *Arabian* groves
> Yields not so sweet an odour: prethee taste it;
> Taste it good *Crocale*; yet I envy thee so great a blessing;
> 'Tis not sin to touch these Rubies, is it? . . .
> Or thus to live *Camelion* like?
> I could resign my essence to live ever thus.
> O welcome; raise him up Gently.
>                                   (II.i.272–276; 279–283, 285–287)

The Amazons are willing to forego their promise to their leader and lay down their lives in order to feel Albert's breath, "touch these Rubies," and rub his skin. In contrast to these beautiful lusty women, Albert manages to resist the temptation to love them—he maintains his vow of fidelity to Aminta—while pretending to love Clarinda in order to acquire food and shelter. The civilized Albert uses his head, while the Amazons, as savage women, are misled by their wild bodily urges.

As a result of the discovery of the European men, Rosellia is forced to allow her women to have their desired sexual contact with them. However, she limits their sexual relations to once a month, and says that if the women should become pregnant, they will be allowed to keep their female children, but must return any male children to their fathers. Rosellia's resolution replicates Columbus's and Raleigh's fantasies as well as classical mythological accounts of Amazons' sexual contact with men.[72] Under Rosellia's savage command, then, traditional seventeenth-century rules of gender and authority are reversed— at least temporarily: women control and colonize and men are the objects of female desire and domination. Rosellia's plan never comes into effect, however, as the women are restored to their European "civilized" identities when they are reunited with Sebastian and Nicusa (Rosellia's husband and nephew). Although Rosellia represents a powerful and potent female voice in seventeenth-century dramatic discourse, she must be reinscribed into the patriarchal ideology at the end of the play.

On the barren side of the island, Sebastian and Nicusa have also gone native, although theirs is not a blessed or prosperous condition. When the pirates first discover the islanders, they do not recognize their former enemies and believe they have encountered monsters or animals. Tibalt asks if Sebastian and Nicusa are "Sea-Calves" and states that they "have horse-tails growing to 'em./ Goodly long manes" (I.i.349,353–354). Aminta wonders if they are "humane creatures" (I.i.348). The Europeans' shock at the sight of Sebastian and Nicusa recalls the Europeans' reaction to Caliban in *The Tempest*. Caliban, similarly, is a "mooncalf" (II.ii.111–112, III.ii.22,23), "strange thing," "fish," and "thing of darkness" (V.i.290,266,275), and he is referred to countless times as a monster. Sebastian counters the French by claiming that Nicusa's and his "miseries [on the island] make us seem monsters" (I.i.365). They are Calibans, therefore, only in appearance, and only for a very brief period during the course of the play; their savage appearance is the result of their victimization.

In contrast to Rosellia and her women, then, the Portuguese noblemen have maintained their civilized natures—even if their physical appearance suggests otherwise. They have formed no new society or social contract, they have not adapted to their physical surroundings, they are unable to find enough food, and unlike Albert, they do not attempt to cross the treacherous river; they wait only for the opportunity to be restored to their natural state of power and privilege. Unlike the women, then, Sebastian's and Nicusa's savagery is not self-chosen, and they do not perceive the island to be "blest"; for them it is a place of "misery." Wildness comes naturally for women, Fletcher suggests, while it is an unnatural burden for the civilized Portuguese noblemen.

Non-aristocratic and lower-class European men, like the woman in the play, are figured as intrinsically wild and savage. After Albert goes off in search of food, the starving French pirates plot to kill and eat Aminta's body. Fletcher's staging of cannibalistic desire is probably based on the period called starving time in the early history of the Virginia Colony, although the direct historical influence is less important than the ideological need to reassert control against the danger of going native. Even the description of how Aminta's body will be eaten and served resembles that of the cannibalization of the woman's body in starving time. Morat asserts that Aminta will not need "powdering," Surat says she "will want salt," and Lamure says that he has read stories "of/Women that have eate their Children,/Men their slaves, nay their brothers: but these are nothing;/Husbands devoured their Wives/ (th[ey] are their Chattels)/And of a Schoolmaster that in a time of famine,/Powdered up all Scholars" (III.i.122,110–115). Men may eat their wives if necessity leads them to it because women are men's property, their "chattel." Fletcher's play emphasizes the comic and sardonic extreme to which the logic of property tends.

Fletcher's Europeans in the wilderness, therefore, like Shakespeare's, need patriarchal and monarchical authority in order to prevent cannibalism, uncontrolled greed, violence, and sexual lasciviousness from overcoming them. Most important to this study, the control of European female bodies is necessary to the restoration of a "civilized" European sociopolitics and monarchical power. When the women-as-land are controlled, in effect, the patriarchal structure is restored. The Pocahontas myth is restaged, therefore, in *The Sea Voyage*. The women in the play represent the fertile land and commodities of the New World and their containment is crucial to the reproduction of future European aristocrats. Sebastian and Nicusa need to reunite with the Portuguese women in order to thrive economically and to (re)produce their lineage.

Rosellia and her Amazons, like Miranda, Caliban, and the absent/present Sycorax in Shakespeare's *Tempest* demonstrate the crisis in performing the other woman onstage in the seventeenth century. The complexities of contemporary English politics and the ambivalent desire of colonial conquest are displaced uneasily onto other European nations and onto a supposedly empty land (empty of "real" native inhabitants). The European Aminta reminds us of Pocahontas—she is abducted and marries her captor, and her union with the Albert ends the dispute between warring French factions. Like Pocahontas, she acts as an emissary of peace for all disparate factions in the play. However, Aminta's European whiteness is a chilling reminder of the now-dead Pocahontas and the 1622 massacre in Virginia which ended the possibility of Native American assimilation through interracial marriage. Aminta is not a Pocahontas at all, in this sense; instead, she represents the idealized, domesticated European woman who the English colonists need to replicate European familial and political structures in Virginia. Powerful Indian women *are* invoked more overtly in the play; indeed, Rosellia discusses the Amazonian part she has adopted as belonging to former women of the Island, but her role-playing only marks (and mocks) English anxieties about Native American women. Rosellia's acting is thus a deliberate ploy, or trick, because she returns to her former self as a subservient wife and noblewoman and ultimately forgoes being Indian. Through Rosellia's performance of otherness, then, Fletcher attempts to demonstrate that real Native Americans do not or have ceased to exist, at least on *this* island. At the same time, Rosellia's Amazonian character asks us to consider whether powerful Native American women do exist, if not here, then maybe somewhere, and thus Fletcher makes Amazons visible in ways that Columbus and Raleigh in all their travels could not. Fletcher's staging of the native women creates presence and absence, fear and longing, paranoia and nostalgia. *The Sea Voyage*, therefore, is a destabilizing mimicry of that which never was, but might be or might have been. Shakespeare's other woman, on the other hand, and the "empty" island his Europeans occupy, efface and deny the presence or necessary murder of Indians which made that emptiness possible. Yet the very silence about Native Americans begs the question it seeks to deny: What made this island "mine"?

# TWO

# Restoration Revisions of *The Tempest*

The adaptations of *The Tempest* that follow Fletcher's *Sea Voyage* were written and performed after the Interregnum. In these plays, the echoes of the socio-politics of *The Tempest* and the political events of the seventeenth century are obvious—usurped kingdoms, rebellious lower classes, and restored thrones.[1] As George Guffey notes, "Shakespeare's play was itself a 'restoration' comedy. That is, it centered on the restoration of the rightful Duke of Milan to the throne that had earlier been wrested illegally from him."[2] The adaptations of *The Tempest* after 1660 explore the cultural anxiety concerning the overthrow of Charles I in the 1640s and the uncertainties of Restoration politics. With the exception of Thomas Durfey's *A Common-Wealth of Women*, patriarchal authority is never fully restored in any of these adaptations. Katherine Eisaman Maus suggests that although the idea of the family and patriarchy as the origin of the state was a significant political weapon for the Stuarts and their allies in the early seventeenth century, "as the century wore on, patriarchalism seemed increasingly nostalgic—an attempt to recover the lost monarchical privilege enjoyed by the early Stuarts." Hence, in Restoration adaptations of *The Tempest*, the figure of the "father-king" becomes "anachronistic."[3] Michael Neill argues similarly that monarchs of Restoration drama oftentimes "prove as corrupt and self-seeking as the revolutionaries who oppose them." The heroic ethos of the pre–civil war Stuarts had faded for royalists, because "it was a past . . . of incompetence, failure, and ultimate defeat, . . . [and for those] whose family allegiances had lain with the Good Old Cause the ignominious collapse of Republican hopes in 1660 rendered any alternative mythology of heroic success equally suspect."[4] For this reason, as Susan Staves puts it, the

Restoration is "the great age of the failed epic."[5] Father-kings and their societies in the drama of the Restoration are morally corrupt, and the line between rebel and legitimate king is thus obscured. As we shall see throughout this chapter, the king's (and father's) power becomes weakened because of his own corruption, and he is unable or unwilling to discipline his daughters and prevent them from going native, that is, living out the desires that had been channeled into "proper" behavior in the plays of the early seventeenth century. In *The Tempests* of the Restoration, Shakespeare's and Fletcher's distinctions between the power of fathers and daughters, and between Europeans and natives, blur.

In the Restoration *Tempests*, the other invades Europe and the European sense of social identity. This reversal of the discourse of colonialism functions dialectically both to disclose the internal corruption of English society and politics and to champion a "new" kind of political power which is imperialistic and nationalistic. Linda Colley argues that, at this time, the English attempted to forge a collective national identity by contrasting themselves to their imperial rivals, especially the French, but also "to the colonial peoples they [the English] conquered, peoples who were manifestly alien in terms of culture, religion and colour."[6] Christopher Hill demonstrates how the attempted consolidation of English identity was effected through significant measures supporting colonization immediately enacted by the crown after Charles II's restoration. In 1661 the legal rate of interest was once again fixed at six percent, and tobacco planting was prohibited within England to promote the interests of colonial expansion. A committee of the Privy Council was created to study and advise on matters of colonial affairs. In 1662, Charles married Catherine de Braganza, whose marriage dowry included a naval base at the gate of the Mediterranean in Tangier and English possession of Bombay in India. Further, the dissolving of proprietary rule in the Caribbean in 1663 and the maintenance of Jamaica under direct governmental control demonstrated that the commonwealth policies in support of expansion were to be continued during the Restoration.[7] The passing of the Navigation Act of 1660 was perhaps the most obvious indication of the Restoration government's initial support of colonization. The 1660 act, David Hawke argues, was "the cornerstone of the English trade and navigation system throughout the rest of the colonial period,"[8] and its subsequent amendments during the Restoration "mark a decisive turning point in England's economic history."[9] By the time of Charles II's death, England was in possession of the whole eastern seaboard of North America, the Hudson Bay Territory, several West Indian Islands, and Bombay on the east coast and Madras on the west coast of India. The East Indian Company was in secure occupation by the authority of the Mogul in India, and it possessed a great trading center at Fort William. By

1668, England was on her way to becoming a powerful European empire, whatever political, ideological, and religious crises the country had endured (and continued to endure) during the last seventy years. In effect, the call for the political and economic investment in expansion diverted English audiences from the problem of the absence of a heroic king and the lack of social and political congruity; it brought the English together in a common purpose. Thus, as Colley demonstrates, imperial expansion represented a means of strengthening the crown's and nation's interests and, hence, potentially uniting the English.[10]

The first of the Restoration redactions of *The Tempest* was *The Enchanted Island*.[11] Dryden's and Davenant's play was first performed in 1667 and first printed in 1670. The plot of *The Enchanted Island* is based on Shakespeare's play, but Dryden and Davenant have added several important characters: Caliban's sister, Sycorax; Miranda's sister, Dorinda; and a white aristocratic male, Hippolito, whom Prospero has raised in complete isolation. As Micheal Dobson notes, in the original production, Hippolito was played by a woman—Moll Davis, which comically undermines the Miltonic assertion that women are born from men and "dramatizes the fact that sexual roles are" constructed.[12] The addition of the female characters weakens Prospero's authority as patriarch: in Shakespeare's play the rebellion on the island is limited to the plot of Caliban, Trinculo, and Stephano; in Dryden's and Davenant's *Enchanted Island* savagery has spread to Prospero's own children and male ward. As Earl Miner points out, in "Shakespeare's version, the sexual threat is that of Caliban against his superior, Miranda. In Dryden's and Davenant's version the threat is among the higher characters themselves."[13] The savagery of Caliban and his mother Sycorax has invaded the Europeans. In particular, the European female characters in *The Enchanted Island* are far more sexually uncontrollable than Shakespeare's Miranda; hence, Prospero's ability to supervise the female body—to keep the wildness of the savage from invading the European woman—is presented as much more limited.[14]

In *The Enchanted Island*, Dorinda functions, at first, as Miranda's other, sexualized self, the wild woman whom Prospero cannot control. Miranda, like seventeenth-century representations of the native Indian, is thus dichotomized as compliant and submissive, and barbarous and sexually lascivious. This division occurs within the white female self, and, in the play, the savage half ultimately takes control of both sisters. In this respect, they become in some measure like Sycorax, the untamed native stand-in, who potentially subverts the power of the patriarch and calls into question the ideology of colonization. In Dryden's and Davenant's version, then, the other female self is no longer the shadow of a dead woman; the unruly native woman is present *within* the

European daughter, and she thus threatens the stability of the whole social order.

The first words Prospero utters in this version are *"Miranda*! where's your Sister?" (I.ii.1)[15] Prospero's lack of knowledge of his daughter's whereabouts highlights his loss of power: from the first moment that he is onstage the audience recognizes his inability to keep the female body within his sight and therefore within his control. Miranda tells Prospero that she left Dorinda "looking from the pointed Rock, at the walks/end, on the huge beat of Waters" (I.ii.2–3). Dorinda cannot be restrained by her father or sister, and she is depicted in implicitly sexualized terms. Prospero responds to this information by calling the phallic "pointed rock" that "dreadful object" as a warning to Miranda of the dangers of sexual desire (I.ii.4). The opening dialogue, then, constructs Prospero's power as always and already undermined; he cannot restrict the female from pursuing her own desires. Dryden and Davenant suggest that, as Miranda's double, Dorinda—and by implication the European woman—cannot discipline herself either.

Dorinda is presented, therefore, as escaping Prospero's supervision and potentially succumbing to the conventional characteristics of the native woman. Not only are the first descriptions of Dorinda saturated with sexual imagery, but the first words she speaks are about sex. In act 1, scene 2, after Prospero confides the history of their family to Miranda (the story of his usurpation and the escape from Mantua) and departs, Dorinda enters. She passionately describes the tempest to Miranda:

> Oh, Sister! what have I beheld? . . .
> From yonder Rock,
> As I my Eyes cast down upon the Seas,
> The whistling winds blew rudely on my face,
> And the waves roar'd; at first I thought the War
> Had bin between themselves, but strait I spy'd
> A huge great Creature . . .
> This floating Ram did bear his Horns above;
> All ty'd with Ribbands, ruffling in the wind,
> Sometimes he nodded down his head a while,
> And then the Waves did heave him to the Moon;
> He clamb'ring to the top of all the Billows,
> And then again he curtsy'd down so low,
> I could not see him: till, at last, all side-long
> With a great crack his belly burst in pieces.
> (I.ii.293,295–300,304–311)

Implicitly at least, Dryden and Davenant comically present the ship as a man in the act of sexual intercourse, and Dorinda is enthralled and captivated by what she has seen. Dorinda, the sexually desirous woman, sets the tone for the depiction of women throughout the play. She exemplifies all of the characteristics which Prospero in Shakespeare's *Tempest* tries to channel into falling in love with the proper man. Moreover, Miranda's self-containment in *The Enchanted Island* is fleeting at best. She gains vicarious pleasure in hearing of the sexualized storm, and she is eager to meet her first man—more so than Dorinda, as we shall later see. She also has her own taboo sexual desires. It is Miranda who informs her sister that "In this great Creature [the ship] there were other Creatures;/And shortly we may chance to see that thing,/Which you have heard my Father call, a Man" (I.ii.315–317). Evidently, Miranda is unconvinced by Prospero that these desires are dangerous or "dreadful."

Dorinda does not know what a man is, and, significantly, it is Miranda who provides her sister with information about the opposite sex. Miranda's explanation and Dorinda's response construct both sisters as unconstrained others who are reminiscent of stereotypical seventeenth-century depictions of Native American women. Miranda says that Prospero has told her that "we Women were made for" man (I.ii.320); Dorinda ironically interprets this to mean that men will "eat" them (I.ii.321), comically linking men with cannibals or animals. Miranda then explains that men will not eat them: "you see my Father is a man, and yet/ He does us good. I would he were not old," to which Dorinda responds, "Methinks indeed it would be finer, if we two had two young Fathers" (I.ii.322–325). Both sisters thus voice an unconscious or barely repressed incestuous desire for the father. The sisters then question their own origin and, hence, their father's authority and power. They thereby evoke in a few lines precisely what Prospero has tried to prevent: a sexual awareness that threatens the transmission of property between families. Dorinda wants to know why they "are not Brothers/then, and have not Beards like" Prospero, and she asks Miranda how Prospero came to be their father (I.ii.328–329). This question, Miranda says, "pose[s]" her (I.ii.330). She explains that "I think he found us when we both were little, and grew/within the ground" (I.ii.332–333). Tellingly, Miranda associates herself with the land (she conflates and confuses the mother's womb with mother earth), even though Prospero has just explained her history to her earlier in act 1, scene 2. She perceives herself as a product of nature, like the gold and minerals in the earth of the New World. While Miranda's story identifies the sisters with a feminized nature, this information leads Dorinda to the conclusion that she can turn the discourse of male domination on its head. She thinks that if their father can dig up women from the earth, perhaps they can do the same and "find some little ones for us/to play with" (I.ii.333–334). Dorinda wants to participate actively in sexual "play" as her father has done. In their discovery of man, then, the sisters find they want lovers of their own, and this desire leads them to rebel against their father's commands.

Just as the addition of Dorinda undermines the father's authority, so too the addition of Hippolito threatens the discourse of monarchical authority in the play. Act 2 revolves around Prospero's futile attempts to keep his lustful daughters and Hippolito from meeting. In part, Prospero's attempted restraint of his children and ward functions ideologically as part of his plan to unite Miranda with Ferdinand and Dorinda with Hippolito. As in Shakespeare's *Tempest*, Prospero's mock restraint of the European lovers is intended to fuel their desire and encourage their "proper" union(s). Yet in *The Enchanted Island*, Prospero's plan goes haywire. Without the help of Ariel, the play would end in chaos.[16]

In act 2, when Prospero finds his daughters walking too closely to where Hippolito remains hidden, he grows upset because they have disobeyed his instructions (II.iv). Prospero reminds them that a "man" resides along the path they tread and that it is "very dangerous" (II.iv.93) to walk there:

*Prospero:* All that you can imagine ill is there,
The curled Lyon, and the rugged Bear
Are not so dreadful as that man.

*Miranda:* Oh me, why stay we here then?

*Dorinda:* I'le keep far enough from his Den, I warrant him.

*Miranda:* But you have told me, Sir, you are a man;
And yet you are not dreadful.

*Prospero:* I child! but I Am a tame man;
old men are tame By Nature,
but all the danger lies in a wild
Young man.

*Dorinda:* Do they run wild about the Woods?

*Prospero:* No, they are wild within Doors, in Chambers,
And in Closets.

*Dorinda:* But Father, I would stroak 'em, and make 'em gentle;
Then sure they would not hurt me.

*Prospero:* You must not trust them, Child: No woman can come
Neer 'em but she feels a pain full nine Months . . .
be you, *Miranda*, your Sister's Guardian.

(II.iv.96–114)

The distinction which Prospero makes between the young "wild man" and himself is that the former is wild because of his youth and sexual potency. In effect, Prospero is "tame" because he is old and therefore implicitly impotent. Prospero's explanation suggests that if he were young, he would be a sexual threat to his own daughters, or, more subtly, he offers a sexual description of his own desire and authority. He states that "wildness" exists within Europeans as well as natives; for Prospero, savagery has more to do with age and gender than race or culture. According to Prospero's theory, he must have been savage once, and Hippolito and Ferdinand are effectively wild men because they are young and sexually desirous. Yet Prospero's account of the difference between himself and a wild man undermines his own power—if the "proper" European ruler is sexually impotent, and also fears the sexuality/fertility of his female subjects, how can he reproduce his own race?

After Prospero leaves his daughters in act 2, scene 2, Miranda takes on the role of the sexual aggressor, the breaker of the father's rules. Dorinda immediately suggests to Miranda that they walk another way to avoid the man who might have "four" legs (II.iv.117). Ironically, it is Miranda who soothes Dorinda's fears, insists that they go against their father's command, and suggests they will not be hurt because they will be able to "spy him [Hippolito] e're he comes too near" (II.iv.129). Miranda continues to walk toward Hippolito's dwelling despite Dorinda's pleas (and despite Prospero's warnings that she "guard" Dorinda), assuring her sister of their safety. Miranda does not follow Prospero's command to guard her sister because she does not guard herself (II.iv.114). When we last saw Miranda in act 1, scene 2, she was still enthralled by the father's "magick;" now she disobeys him by pursuing her desires and encourages Dorinda to collude with her in this disobedience.

Prospero saved Hippolito, the heir to the dukedom of Mantua, and brought him to the island years earlier. Hippolito thus functions as Ferdinand's (or Prospero's) dark double: he is an aristocratic European gone native. Like Caliban in Shakespeare's version, Hippolito is confined to a cave, so that he will not impregnate Prospero's daughter(s). Unlike Caliban, however, he has been taught to read. In order to keep Hippolito from his daughters, Prospero tells him that women are "enemies" (II.iv.31) and that they are "Fatally beauteous, and have killing Eyes;/Their voices charm beyond the Nightingales;/They are all enchantment: those, who once behold 'em,/Are made their slaves for ever" (II.iv.46–49). Hippolito understandably is too provoked not to look and act when the opportunity arises.

Although Hippolito comes to love Dorinda once they meet, this passion leads him, like an uncivilized Caliban, to want all women. His savage desire demonstrates Prospero's weakness as a ruler; his white male ward, like his white daughters, has become wild. Apparently, Prospero has not been successful in teaching him about monogamy and marriage, and Hippolito's wildness threatens to destroy his guardian's plan altogether. After Ferdinand falls in love with

Miranda, Prospero imprisons him in the same cave as Hippolito—pretending to keep both men away from the sisters whom he actually intends them to marry. While they are imprisoned, Ferdinand informs Hippolito that there are other women besides Dorinda in the world, but explains that each man is allowed only one woman. Hippolito does not understand why he cannot have all the wives he wants; he believes that "This Stranger [Ferdinand] does insult and comes into my/World to take those heavenly beauties from me" (III.vi.93–94), and their dispute results in a duel. Hippolito is positioned as a polygamous heathen of the island, and their duel stages in microcosm the history of the colonization of the New World. Apologists for empire claimed that natives were primitives who needed to be Christianized and saved, and this supposedly justified the destruction of the native Indian people and their cultures. Yet, as Hippolito also reminds us, the English colonists did indeed come into the New World, the Indian's world, not only to save the savage, but "to take those heavenly beauties" from the natives—those beauties include land, minerals, furs, crops, women, and men. Like the native, then, Hippolito questions the right of the European Ferdinand to impose his laws and rules upon the indigenous peoples' lands and cultures.

The fight between Hippolito and Ferdinand, like the fight between Indians and Europeans, leads to the taming of the native and the assertion of colonial authority. Hippolito dies in the duel with Ferdinand because he does not know how to fight with a sword; like the seventeenth-century natives, he is overpowered by European technology and know-how. However, at the end of the play Ariel—on his own initiative—magically restores Hippolito to life, and, as a result, all of the love matches are saved. Through his defeat and death, Hippolito learns to accept monogamy. The patrilineal morality which Ferdinand defends is portrayed ultimately as more powerful than Hippolito's uncivilized desires. The European tames the white man gone native in Dryden's and Davenant's vision, and colonial power is reaffirmed. Hippolito is now fit to return to Mantua and to take back his dukedom.

Yet with Hippolito as Duke of Mantua, the wildness of the New World seems awfully close to home. The lines between savage and civilized are ambiguous; Hippolito is a former wild man who was raised in a cave on an island, yet he is also a European duke. "If Shakespeare's *Tempest* obsessively expels the matriarchal and polices the female," as Dobson points out, with Hippolito played by a woman, "this aspect of its Restoration variant stages their revenge."[17] *Female* chaos of the New World, then, invades the European court: a woman will marry a woman, and a woman will be duke. In addition, Hippolito's transgressive act of double cross-dressing (the actress as man, the woman/man as native) in the original production of this *Tempest*, further calls into questions such categories as patriarchy, gender, and race.[18]

Dryden and Davenant add another significantly unruly character who creates a radical ambivalence in the strategy of repressing the native woman, Sycorax, Caliban's sister. While in Shakespeare's play Sycorax, the female "monster hag," is dead, Dryden and Davenant bring Sycorax, the "freckled hag-born [whelp] . . . not honoured with a human shape" on stage. Shakespeare, in effect, effaces the black woman by killing her off before the play begins. Though Dryden's and Davenant's Sycorax is portrayed as a buffoon, she nevertheless remains visible and audible, and, hence, the native woman and all that she represents cannot be entirely destroyed by white male power. She is large, loud, and animalistic. Caliban describes her as an animal, "clambring up a hollow Oak,/ And plucking thence the dropping Honey-Combs" (II.iii.203–204). Sycorax is identified with the wilderness itself. Notably, in his comic rebellion against royal authority, Trincalo takes Sycorax as his wife because he believes that by marrying her he inherits all rights to the island; he tells Mustacho and Ventoso that he is their ruler because he has "Espous'd the lawful Inheritrix of this Island, / Queen *Blouze* the first, and having homage done me, / By this hectoring Spark her Brother, from these two/ I claim a lawful Title to this Island" (III.iii.119–122). Through the character of Sycorax, then, Dryden and Davenant comically vent anxieties about dynastic succession and legitimacy, brought to the fore by the civil war.

Yet Sycorax, though present and alive in Davenant's and Dryden's play, is only a mock-version of her mother in Shakespeare's *Tempest*, and she is merely a stand-in for the absent "original" owners of the island, the Native Americans who are never spoken of directly or represented on stage in Shakespeare's *Tempest* or in *The Enchanted Island*. In contrast to the mother for whom she is a substitute, the young Sycorax appears to possess no magic or power; she is merely a lecherous idiot. Only the lower-class drunken sailors are seduced by Sycorax, and even they know they are committing a devilish crime by having sex with her. Trincalo only reluctantly gives in to Sycorax's pleas that he sleep with her. Sycorax's behavior might be seen as a burlesque imitation of the native women's pursuit of the prudish John Smith in "The Virginia Mask," as Trincalo at first strongly repudiates her advances. Trincalo, like Smith, is disgusted by the native woman, but like John Rolfe, he also sees the economic advantages of such a union.

At the end of the play, "all past crimes" are "bur[ied]" (V.ii.151). Prospero frees Ariel and forgives his brother Antonio for having usurped his throne; Hippolito and Dorinda, and Ferdinand and Miranda, are to be married, and Alonzo restores the dukedom of Mantua to Hippolito. The drunken and foolish rebels—Trincalo, Mustacho, and Ventriculo—are discovered before their comic plot to kill Prospero comes to fruition, and Caliban willingly submits to Prospero. Caliban learns to recognize his true master—the upper class European man; he no longer complains of Prospero's treatment of him or demands his freedom. Yet, in the final act, Sycorax is prevented from returning to Europe with Trincalo as she desires. When she begs Trincalo to let her go with him on the voyage back to Mantua, he replies, "No, my dainty Dydapper, you have a tender constitution, and will be sick a Ship-board. You are partly Fish and may swim after me. I wish you a good voyage" (V.ii.251–253). Trincalo's comical suggestion that Sycorax is not fit for travel on a ship because she is too "dainty" seems absurd given what we know about her size and constitution; he clearly does not want her aboard the ship because she is too monstrous. Sycorax does not insist on going with Trincalo, but remains silent after his suggestion that she swim after him because she is part fish. The play ends then, in part, with the (humorous) repression of the unruly black woman. However, Sycorax may be pregnant—she has probably had sexual intercourse with Trincalo, Stephano, and Caliban (Trincalo says he found her "singing Tory, Rory,/ and Ranthum, Scantum, with her own natural Brother" [IV.ii.108–109])—and that possibility presents an ambivalence in the sociopolitical discourse of the play. The (potential) life in her womb symbolizes the uncertainty of the absolute power of the royal patriarch to control the female native (or black surrogate). In contrast to Shakespeare's Caliban, Sycorax may indeed people the island with a hybrid race.

Like Shakespeare's *Tempest*, Dryden's and Davenent's version of the play also reiterates the slippage of signifiers in staging race and gender. Indeed, the metaphoric referents are so confused it is hard to comprehend who is representing whom, especially as the play itself is an imitation of Shakespeare's *Tempest. The Enchanted Island* both mocks Shakespeare's version and mocks the effects of colonization on English culture. All lines of cultural and gendered distinctions are confused—women act like men, men act like women, women act like stereotypes of Native American and black women, men act like stereotypes of Native Americans as well, and black people act like and stand in for stereotypes of Native Americans. The slippage of sign and signifier in performing all characters is extreme, perhaps deliberately so, and we might say this is what makes the play a comedy. Yet the comedy also reminds us quite seriously that the cultures and genders are blurring dangerously and perversely in colonial expansion. More important, perhaps, the comedy seeks to mask the unrepresentable Native Americans, who by this time in coastal North American history were being exterminated and driven off their land.

Ironically, the comedy does represent a black woman—Sycorax the buffoon—at a point in history when English engagement with the slave trade was at full tilt. Sycorax's portrayal would fit well with Kathleen M. Brown's assessment of the black women in Virginia in the late seventeenth century, as I discussed in the Introduction. Brown contends that black women were perceived and portrayed as mindless drudges who deserved to be enslaved and who could function effectively as much needed agricultural laborers in a tobacco economy. The reproduction of the young Sycorax's children, then, would not be viewed as a threat. Indeed, Sycorax's future slave children would enable the colonial project and its profit to grow exponentially. By mating Sycorax with other white male fools or with Caliban, moreover, the playwrights do not allow her to swallow up the authority or the family name of the European noblemen—their "lower-class" seed is necessary only for the production of laborers in the colony anyway. Sycorax is important to this play, then, because in contrast to the lone male Caliban in Shakespeare's version, her sexuality does not completely disturb the European social order. Like the black female slaves in Virginia who enable white women to leave the tobacco fields and help their husbands to rise socially, Sycorax's body and her reproductive capacity enables the white women in this *Tempest* to retain their racial and class purity and remain as vessels for future noble European heirs and the transmission of property.

Thomas Duffet's *The Mock-Tempest*, "one of the funniest parodies in English literature," opened in 1674, not long after the opening of Thomas Shadwell's operatic version of *The Tempest*.[19] *The Mock-Tempest's* humor lies in its undermining of the ideology of patrilineal authority and the concomitant scapegoating of the native woman. In this version, the fatherly figure is repeatedly mocked, traditional hierarchies of class and gender are overturned, and the savagery of the New World symbolically invades England. While in earlier versions the New World had served as a safe and distant testing ground for displaying and containing tensions within England's social disorder, in Duffet's play the savagery represented by the female native can no longer be held at bay. The uncontainable sexual chaos of the native woman overpowers England and the patriarchal authority of Old World is turned comically upside down.

In *The Mock-Tempest*, there is no patriarchal figure of authority who retains the power to stabilize civil misrule in England. As Ariel sings to Quakero (previously Ferdinand) "Thy Daddies dead, thy Daddies dead" (III.ii.44),[20] suggesting that the discourse of monarchical and fatherly authority is also destroyed. Quakero's comical name overtly travesties the discourse of patriarchal authority in the play. Female Quakers were outspoken and possessed freedoms among their sect that non-Quaker women did not. The Quakers were also stereotyped in seventeenth-century drama as hypocrites, particularly sexual hypocrites. Quakers are made the butt of numerous jokes throughout *The Mock-Tempest*. For example, a female Quaker named "Fraud" in act 2, scene 2, is sent by Ariel to torment Alonzo and Antonio; and Fraud sings: "With upright look, and speech sincere,/ In publick, I a Saint appear./ But in private

I put out the light,/And I serve for a Whore, or a Baud./ I have taught them to cheat,/ Swear, and Fight,/ For by Yea, and by Nay, I am a Fraud" (II.ii.125–130). Thus not only is the future Duke Quakero's role symbolically turned upside down because of the political associations of his name, but his royal title is undermined as well. The notably female Quaker with whom he is linked is a self-proclaimed hypocrite, liar, fraud, whore, and bawd.

Ironically, the dukedom Prospero has lost is the "Lord Mayors Dogg-kennel," and he is now "Keeper of Bridewell," a prison for prostitutes (I.ii.20–21,23). Prospero is now a pimp, and his daughters are prostitutes. His profession in Duffet's play mocks Shakespeare's version of the courtship narrative; in Shakespeare's *Tempest*, Prospero mates his daughter with Ferdinand, while Duffet's version implies that the mating of people is not far from the breeding of dogs. In Prospero's recitation about the family history to Miranda, he explains that he lost his "weighty state" because his brother, "having learned the mysterious Craft of coupling Doggs, and untying them" usurped him, and "Suck'd out all my Juice" (I.ii.42–44,49). His brother then betrayed Prospero to Alonzo, "Duke of Newgate"—another prison—and, "in a stormy dreadfull Night open'd [his] Kenell Gates, and forc'd [him] thence with thy young Sister, and thy howling self [Miranda]" (I.ii.52–54). Prospero says they were saved from death because of "the love my dogged Subject bore me" (I.ii.56–57). His statement that Miranda was "howling" on the night of their departure, as well as the pun on "dogged Subject," suggests that Prospero's daughter and subjects may be beasts. It is not clear whether Miranda is human or animal; in fact, like Caliban and Sycorax (in the Dryden and Davenant *Tempest*), the implication is that she is both.

Not only is Prospero presented as a former keeper of a dog kennel and a pimp to his own daughters, but his magical powers are limited to thievery and rabble-rousing. When Ariel flies to assist Prospero in act 1, scene 2, he says, "Hayl most potent Master, I come to serve thy pleasure/Be it to lye, swear, steal, pick pockets, or creep in at Windows" (I.ii.77–78). Ariel then describes the tempest he has created for Prospero:

> I gather'd the Rabble together, show'd them the Bawdy House, told 'em they us'd to kill Prentices, and make mutton pyes of 'em. . . . Then I ran and call'd the Constable, who came just as the Rabble broke in, and the defendents were leaping from the Balcony, like Saylers from a sinking Ship. The Duke and his Trayn I clap'd into a Coach.
>
> (I.ii.80–87)

The Prospero of *The Mock-Tempest* is ironically engaged in encouraging civil misrule. In this version of *The Tempest*, it is the usurped father who is responsible for the political division and social disorder which Shakespeare's Prospero tries to contain. England and the wild, untamed island in the New World are satirically conflated.

*The Mock-Tempest* opens to cries of "Whore, a Whore" amidst the clamor of breaking of windows and doors of a brothel (I.i). While Davenant and Dryden had highlighted the sexual aspects of the storm through Dorinda's impassioned observation of it, in Duffet's play the "tempest" is an attack of the wild "rabble" upon a whorehouse in England. Symbolically, the "rabble" of men are the wild sea, the whorehouse is the ship, and the prostitutes are the mutinous sailors. Gonzalo says that the chaos is "More noyle and terrour then a Tempest at Sea" (I.i.65), and Stephania, the "mother" bawd, calls the other women "Seditious mutiners" (I.i.52,63). Like the native woman in earlier versions of *The Tempest*, the prostitutes—to whom Stephania refers as "Amazons"—are presented as licentious monsters who are dangerous to men (I.i.19). The prostitutes, accused of killing "prentices" and making them into pies, embody the negative characteristics of the native, cannibalistically as well as sexually.

The body of European woman in *The Mock-Tempest* is associated with the economic system of mercantile trade between Europe and America. The "many-headed-monster-Multitude" who attack the brothel offer peace in exchange for gaining profit from the prostitutes' trade, and their trade is linked symbolically to colonial mercantilism (I.i.134). The "plentipotentiary" offers peace on the following terms:

> First, they demand the Dominion of the Straights Mouth, and all the Mediterranean Sea—That every Frigot, Fireship, you have, Shall strike, furle up their sail, and lye by to the least of their Cock-boats, where-ever they meet, and receive a man aboard to search for prohibited Goods, and permit him to romage fore and oft without resistance. . . . Secondly, That all their Vessels shall have and enjoy a free-trade into and out of all your Ports without paying any Custom. . . . Lastly, That you re-imburse the charge of the War, pay for the Cure of the wounded, and the recov'ry of those that have surfeited on your rotten Ling and Poys'nous Oyl, and allow Pensions for those that are dismember'd—What say ye, Peace, or War?
>
> (I.i.138–147,153–157)

The Plenipotentiary's "demand" implicitly refers to the 1651 Navigation Act and its subsequent amendments during the Restoration. These acts were intended to "subordinate the colonies, to maintain the merchant navy, and to deprive the Dutch of the carrying trade between Asia and England."[21] As a result of the acts, England became engaged in North American and Indian trade.[22] But the acts also caused numerous wars, as the prostitutes' response to the plenipotentiary's demands remind us: three wars with the Dutch (one during the Interregnum, two during the Restoration), civil wars within the colonies, as well as civil wars within England between advocates of mercantilism and colonialism and those whose economic interests were in conflict with expansionist policies. Religious and political dissention which persisted throughout Charles II's and James II's reigns led, as Michael McKeon suggests, to the Exclusion Crisis and the Glorious Revolution.[23]

In *The Mock-Tempest*, Duffet critiques colonialism; he suggests that the entire project is corrupt and destructive to English national power. In Duffet's play, the female body is conflated with the economy of mercantilism: the prostitute is constituted variously as the ships, the sea, the products, and colonial taxes.[24] The cries of "whore" are the first words we hear in act 1, and the cries of "war" are conflated with the prostitute. The prostitute is asked to relinquish her profits, and to offer free goods, or go to war. The prostitutes respond to the Plenipotentiary's demand with a determined cry of "War, War, War" (I.i.159). The crisis of civil strife and economic expansion within England is implicitly blamed on the European woman: the sexual channels of her unchaste body have led to the invasion of otherness and resulted in England's internal anarchy. As the female body's passageway becomes heavily trafficked, like the sea between the colonies and England, the pure English identity becomes invaded by the wild native woman-as-land and the products of the New World. The desecrated female body is constructed as the primary site of violence, savagery, and economic greed in Restoration England.

It is not surprising, then, that Miranda and her double, Dorinda, are prostitutes. Shakespeare's preservation of the father's authority through his control of his daughter's body is turned upside down in *The Mock-Tempest*. Like the Sycorax in Dryden's and Davenant's *Tempest*, these sisters are animalistic, licentious, and anarchic. In contrast to the innocent though desiring Miranda and Dorinda of Dryden's and Davenant's *Enchanted Island*, the sisters are sexually experienced whores. In act 2, scene 1, they explain how it is husbands that are new to them (in place of "men," as in the *The Enchanted Island*), and husbands they intend to exploit and to cuckold. Husbands will take care of their children, provide them with material comfort, while, as Miranda says being their "slaves" (II.i.22). Indeed, Miranda points out, a husband provides better than a father does and can protect her and her progeny from poverty and social exclusion. Yet, the sisters comically declare, if their father does not provide them with "Husbands quickly,/wee'l make [Prospero] lye with us himself" (II.i.48–49). This statement makes explicit the innuendo about incest in *The Enchanted Island*. For Duffet, then, virtue and aristocratic values are reduced to sexual hypocrisy and convenience.

*The Mock-Tempest* thus travesties Shakespeare's discourse in which the sexual purity of the white female body is preserved to ensure the restoration of political authority. Duffet suggests that there is no spotless female body left in English culture of his age, and that all women are whores. This view is the satiric underside of the patrilineal obsession with female chastity and legitimate succession of property and rank. For Shakespeare, Prospero profits from his daughter's union with Ferdinand, but he does so by limiting her contact with Caliban and controlling her relationship with Ferdinand—saving her virginity for the marriage night. Duffet's Prospero, in contrast, earns profit from selling his daughters' bodies not once but many times. His play, then, implies that the restoration of royal authority through the containment of the female body is unattainable, because women, whether non-European or European, are inherently corrupt. Not only are women sexually licentious, Duffet suggests, but also greedy and self-serving. These women who have gone native bear responsibility for the corruption derived from colonial expansion, and they represent the potential chaos within all English men and women.

The representation of race and gender in this play is obviously grafted onto white, poor, working-class women and on the problematic of filling the colonies with prisoners who construct a body politic. Here, the crisis in representation and the problem of surrogation are figured in terms which deny people of color altogether—they are so fully and repeatedly displaced that the colonial racial context is almost obliterated within the play's obsessive concern for the containment of the English woman's body. One might say that the island cannot work at this point in history for the drama because the problem of intercultural relations are so complex that they cannot be represented. Or, one might say, as Kathleen M. Brown's research on Virginia shows us, that the patriarchal political order in the colony repeatedly, anxiously, and obsessively attempts to assert itself through the ideal of the domestic white wife.

The last of the Restoration adaptations of *The Tempest* is *A Common-Wealth of Women*, by Thomas Durfey, licensed in 1685 and printed in 1686. Durfey's play is a close adaptation of Fletcher's *The Sea Voyage*. In striking contrast to *The Mock-Tempest*, Durfey's *A Common-Wealth of Women* looks back nostalgically to the pre–civil war era, and attempts, as Neill argues in a different context, to create a mythology of "Restoration in the largest sense of that potent term."[25] Indeed, Durfey's revision *of The Sea Voyage* emphasizes, rather then undermines, the importance of the patriarchal figure in the play. Like Shakespeare's *Tempest* and Fletcher's *Sea Voyage*, the return of the father in *A Common-Wealth of Women* establishes harmony in the political and familial order. Notably, Durfey's revision was written during a particularly heightened period of crisis concerning royal authority. The Duke of Monmouth's rebellion occurred in 1685, the same year that *A Common-Wealth of Women* was licensed, and the turmoil of the Exclusion Crisis had just passed in 1683. Fletcher's *Sea Voyage* may have seemed like fresh material for Durfey's royalist purposes—the promotion of James II's right of succession—considering the undermining of patriarchal authority in the revisions of Shakespeare's *Tempest* during the Restoration.

One significant change which highlights the role of the patriarch in Durfey's *Common-Wealth of Women* is the simplification of the familial and class relations. There is one father, Sebastian, one noble son, Nicusa, and all of the noble European women are related to Sebastian by marriage or blood—Rosellia is his wife and Clarinda and Aminta are his daughters. Aminta's abduction— her "rape"—and reunification with her family are thus more directly related to the restoration of the noble patriarch.

Another significant change in this version is the alteration of nationalistic affiliations. The play opens in England, not at sea. The first "tempest" in this play is the fight between the Captain and La Mure over Aminta at the end of act 1; symbolically, this is a battle between England and France. Broadly speaking, in *A Common-Wealth of Women*, and corresponding to the general political climate of the 1680s, the French are villains, the Portuguese are victims of French barbarity, and the English (except for the fops who turn savage) are saviors who restore political order in the New World. The battle between the French fathers has thus been eliminated; there is only one French pirate in this version, La Mure, and he has no children. The pirate La Mure is a "villain" who had invaded the Portuguese family's plantations and divided the family sixteen years prior to the opening of the play. Moreover, La Mure keeps company with "disguis'd Turks" (I.i.450) in England[26] and is seized by the Constable under the pretence of his being a Moslem. The Frenchman is presented as a dangerous oriental who abducts a noble white virgin and, hence, threatens European civility. In contrast to Fletcher's play, Aminta chooses her lover and husband in this play—Marine, the Englishman who saves her from La Mure and restores her to her family—rather than coming to love the pirate who has "raped" her, as she does in Fletcher's play.

Another striking alteration in Durfey's version is the overt association of the Portuguese family's destruction with the ideology of woman-as-colonial-product. In *The Sea Voyage*, while the entire family went to sea to escape the pirates and were separated by gender in a storm (with the jewels by indirect means ending up with the men), in this version the women are literally abandoned by Sebastian and Nicusa when the men go off in a ship to save the family's fortune. When attacked by the villainous La Mure, Don Sebastian and his son Nicusa escaped with their fortunes, "and a Party of Negro Slaves," planning to return for the women later (I.i.51,59). Apparently, Sebastian and Nicusa valued their jewels more than their wife, mother, and sisters. La Mure, not knowing "how to pursue" Sebastian and Nicusa (I.i.68), "turn'd his Rage upon [Aminta's] poor Mother, . . . sister, and . . . self./And having Laden his Ship with the Spoils and Riches of our Island, carried [the women] with him, and then put to Sea" (I.i.69–72). Aminta is presented as the pirate's ultimate reward; La Mure keeps her with him and leaves the rest of Portuguese women on an abandoned island. When Marine later rescues Aminta from the French pirate, she is again figured as a commodity; the Lieutenant Du Pier calls her Marine's "Treasure," and Boldsprite, the Ship's Master, states, " 'Sbud, would I had her weight in Tobacco or Pepper" (I.i.376,400). Aminta's body is therefore symbolically, and by this time traditionally, conflated with colonial products.

Like Fletcher, Durfey also suggests that greed, which is figured as the unlawful desire of the grasping middle class, leads white men to go native. When Aminta, Marine, and his crew discover the unrecognizable Sebastian and Nicusa, Sebastian offers the English their fortune in exchange for passage off of the island. But, he warns,

[t]his Gold, was the overthrow of my happiness. For
landing here with a party of Negro-Slaves,
That I commanded to assist me against the Pyrates:
This cursed Gold enticing 'em, they set upon me, and
my Son here;
wounded us almost to Death.

(II.i.443–448)

Yet while Sebastian briefly acknowledges that gold led to his unhappiness, he ironically blames his misery not on his own covetousness but on that of the "Negro-Slaves." He explains that his slaves died in their fight over gold. As a result of the slaves' deaths, Sebastian and Nicusa are left to fend for themselves in the wilderness, and, without their slaves to work for them, Sebastian and Nicusa have had little success in recreating the conditions of their lost plantations. Like the early colonists in Virginia who refused to work to produce their own food, Sebastian and Nicusa nearly starve in the wilderness without others to labor for them. Aristocratic honor effectively prevents them from working.

As in Fletcher's *Sea Voyage*, the Amazon women are depicted as prelapsarian women who live in a fertile land. Yet Durfey's European women in the wild are less of a threat to patriarchal authority than the Amazons of Fletcher's *Sea*

*Voyage*. Durfey's pastoral native women are overtly domesticated. For example, when the Amazons first appear onstage they are singing—joined together in a joyous celebration of their independence and freedom. Yet their song hardly seems as threateningly savage as Marine anticipates when he hears the sounds of their drums from afar. The Amazons are seated comfortably in "a Grotto, and Rosy Bower, plac'd in the midst of a pleasant Country." Nature on the female side of the island is not only fertile, as in Fletcher's play, but also tamed—a garden rather than a jungle (IV.i.76). Although these European women have adopted the customs of their Amazon forebears, they are still described as "Ladies" (58). Rosellia's rebellion against male tyranny is thus softened in Durfey's version of the play.

As if to emphasize the validity of Rosellia's claim concerning male oppression, the European men who travel with Marine to the New World—Frugal, Hazard, and Franville—are notably misogynistic throughout the play, much more so than the the the men who accompany Albert in Fletcher's *Sea Voyage*. Frugal, Hazard, and Franville have gone to sea to escape their wives. When faced with having to mate with the Amazon women, they are visibly angered. Hazard says, "And Have we then, like Flounders, leapt out of the Frying-Pan into the Fire: Fled from a Female Fiend or two at home, to be plagu'd here with a whole Nation of Devils?" (IV.i.151–154). While the men regard the Amazons as devils, the women ironically call the men "chickens" that need to be fattened (IV.i.202). Juliet says the men "are fearful . . . And/like poor Dogs, adore the ground I go on; when I frown, they /hang their Tails, like fearful sheep-hounds—show 'em a Crust of bread, they'l Saint me presently./ Frisk up and down, and skip about like Apes;/And for a drop of Wine, be whipt like Hackney's./ I can saddle 'em, ride 'em—do what I will with 'em" (V.ii.216–226). Further, the males are given traditionally female tasks, such as washing, sowing, spinning, and they are watched over by "Waiters" with "Whips" (99). Ironically, their new role as slaves to the Amazons causes them to miss their wives and presumably their traditional male roles as lords and masters.

With the patriarch-father Sebastian's return at the end of the play, Rosellia concludes that, like the end of the Commonwealth era in England, "times are alter'd now, so is the Government, Whilst my Sebastian lives: 'Tis he must rule it" (V.ii.500–501). Moreover, Aminta's role in the reconstitution of the noble family is much more significant for Durfey: without her, Sebastian says that his "joys" at his family's reunion cannot be "perfect" (V.ii.339). Like Shakespeare's Miranda, therefore, Aminta is the agent through whom the family's wounds are healed. She is "[t]he infant that La Mure carry'd away with him,/When he left [the Portuguese] alone upon this Island,/She has bin bred in England" (V.ii.373–378). Aminta has been raised in England, saved by the English, and she loves an English man; she therefore represents the potential for colonial profit to become the means through which to heal sociopolitical divisions in England.

In this final adaptation of Shakespeare's *Tempest*, the crisis in the performance of race and gender is repeated in much the same way as in the earlier versions: English national identities and politics are diverted onto other European cultures, European women play Amazons and give up their roles at the end of the play, no real Amazons exist in the time frame of the play, white men turn wild and cannabalistic, and although black men are named, they die before the play begins. The problem of representing race and gender, then, is repeated and restaged, and the fictionality of the Native American woman is again underscored. Nonetheless, her absence/presence begs the questions asked throughout the last two chapters: if white women have become other by learning the ways of the Indian woman, what happened to the Amazon woman? Where did she go? And if she is worth imitating, parodying, or mocking, why is she killed off? Or, is she?

The seventeenth-century revisions and adaptations of *The Tempest* examined in chapters 1 and 2 bridge the various stages of England's relationship to colonial expansion throughout the century. For Shakespeare, the repression of the female native on the island in the New World serves as a means of reasserting royal authority in England. The female body is contained, the other is controlled, and the father's power is, for the most part, maintained. However, as the discourses of "restoration" become increasingly challenged throughout the century, so too *The Tempest* changes. In the Restoration adaptations of *The Tempest*, the European daughter is no longer absolutely held within her father's power, the non-European threatens to rebel against political authority, and the father himself is oftentimes corrupt. Each of the authors whom I have examined in chapters 1 and 2 casts his version of *The Tempest* in a different political light, yet each of these plays attempts to unite the divisions in English political discourse over the bodies of the absent/present Indian or black woman, or the body of the European woman who has gone native. Patriarchal authority and the promotion of English expansion are asserted through the colonization of the woman-as-land in the New World. *The Tempest* and its revisions serve, therefore, as crucial texts in the dramatization of English colonization and its attendant tensions and anxieties. As we shall see in the following chapters, the themes of *The Tempest* are again and again reworked and revised. Because the effort to reconstruct a masculinist national identity depends on controlling the native woman-as-land and the containment of female desire, this project is always in the process of falling apart, always in the process of failing. The repeated slippage in the performance of women—black, Indian, white—shows us how complex, ambivalent, and impossible it was and is to perform the woman-as-land metaphor and to contain and repress female power on the seventeenth-century English stage.

# THREE

# The Indian Queen and The Indian Emperour

John Dryden's collaboration with Robert Howard on *The Indian Queen* (1664) and its sequel, *The Indian Emperour* (1665), by Dryden alone, project the politics of imperialism and colonial discourse onto late seventeenth-century dramatic constructions of sex, love, and honor. Like *The Tempest* and its seventeenth-century redactions, *The Indian Queen* and *The Indian Emperour* appropriate Indian culture as a strategy for overcoming political and ideological instability in England. Dryden's representation of the colonization of the Native American land and culture dramatizes the need to eradicate or at least control the wildness within the English man. During the Restoration, foreign expansion and trade held the promise of strengthening and unifying the English nation by increasing its economic as well as military power.[1] Significantly, Dryden portrays the destruction of native culture ambivalently: Montezuma is no monstrous or barbaric Caliban, but a mimic of the qualities of an idealized English nobility. Other than his heroic son, Guyomar, however, Montezuma's Indian subjects are rebellious and self-serving. And, with the exception of Cortes,[2] the Spanish conquerors are portrayed as greedy, ambitious, and inhumane. Nevertheless, it is the Spanish Cortes who ultimately represents the ideal ruler in the play, and the colonization of the New World is presented as politically necessary and morally correct. The crucial difference between the two heroes lies in their relationships to the native woman: Cortes is able to resist her powers and to maintain self-control, while Montezuma is obsessed by his desire for the Indian Princess, and this passion causes him to lose his head and his kingdom. In this respect, the blame for the fall of Mexico is deflected from the colonizers and Montezuma onto the Indian Princess.

As in his collaborative rewriting of *The Tempest*, Dryden's ambivalence regarding the supremacy of the Old World over the New is resolved over the body of the native woman; she bears responsibility for the fall of her native culture because she embodies all that must be expelled in order to make way for the ideal hierarchical relationship between the monarch and his subjects. The Indian woman in *The Indian Queen* and *The Indian Emperour*, like the wild woman in the seventeenth-century *Tempests*, is sexually lascivious and unruly, a Circe-like barbarian who corrupts men's judgment and threatens their honor. She is a symbol of the wilderness of the New World which needs and wants to be tamed. Because the Indian land and culture are feminized and presented as both wild and desirable, Dryden's two plays suggest that the female native and her kingdom must be controlled in order to be exploited. In presenting the native culture as female, fallen, and corrupt, then, Dryden like many of his predecessors, justifies the Western appropriation and economic exploitation of Native American culture and the land of the New World, and he suggests that this effort is politically regenerative for both colonizer and colonized.

Critics have commented extensively on Dryden's ambivalent portrayal of the native Indians and the Spanish conquistadors' conquest of the natives in *The Indian Queen* and *The Indian Emperour*, yet they do not acknowledge what is at stake for the native people and, in particular, the native woman, in Dryden's portrayal of the fall of Mexico. For example, James Anderson Winn aptly argues that the conquest of Mexico is figured in sexualized terms, yet he suggests that for Dryden, the feminine is positive.[3] Jacqueline Pearson suggests that Dryden " 'allies himself with the feminist side in the debate over women's equality'. . . . [He] is fascinated with powerful women."[4] While Joseph Roach takes a complex and astute look at the "circum-atlantic" and intercultural racial relations in *The Indian Emperour*, he, too, fails to fully acknowledge the significance of the fate of the native women in the play.[5] Indeed, none of Dryden's critics examine the implications of reducing the colonization of Mexico to a tragic love story.[6] Often they reproduce a discourse which implicitly lays the blame on the native woman and her people for bringing disaster upon themselves. In contrast to this earlier criticism, I shall explore Dryden's version of the conquest of Mexico from the standpoint of the native woman in order to demonstrate that in Dryden's version of the colonization of Mexico, the construction of the female other as the source of the fall of the native people supports a system of economic exploitation of New World natives. By displacing the responsibility for the evils of colonialism and the extermination of Native Americans onto the Spanish conquistadors, Dryden assuages English guilt and reduces the threat Indians pose to English culture. In Dryden's version of colonization, the natives are always and already doomed.

Dryden's identification of the native woman with the fall of Mexico and his depiction of the feminized land of America as both virginal and corrupt draw on a tradition that goes back to Cortes's Indian translator and lover—La Malinche or Malintzin, as she was called by the Indians, or Dona Marina, as she was called by the Spaniards. The tradition of the Indian woman who betrays her country for the love of the Spanish conquistador is best explained by Cherrie Moraga:

> As translator and strategic advisor and mistress to the Spanish conqueror of Mexico, Hernan Cortes, Malintzin is considered the mother of the mestizo people. But unlike La Virgen de Guadalupe, she is not revered as the Virgin Mother, but rather slandered as La Chingada, meaning the "fucked one," or La Vendida, sell-out to the white race.
>
> Upon her shoulders rests the full blame for the "bastardization" of the indigenous people of Mexico. To put it in its most base terms: Malintzin, also called Malinche, fucked the white man who conquered the Indian peoples of Mexico and destroyed their culture. Ever since, brown men have been accusing her of betraying her race, and over the centuries continue to blame her entire sex for this "transgression."[7]

Moraga points out that, from the Mestizo perspective, Marina takes the blame for the fall of Mexico. Although Spanish historians, such as Francisco Lopez de Gomara and Bernal Diaz, glorify Marina for leading Spain into prosperity, like the Mestizo men, they effectively lay the blame for the destruction of the Indians at Marina's feet. In examining Dryden's plays, we need to consider Marina precisely because she is figured, from the European perspective, as crucial to the conquest of the Mexican people and their land. As Stephen Greenblatt points out, Marina "was the figure in whom all communication between the two opposed cultures [Spanish and Aztec] was concentrated."[8] Although Dryden does not directly recreate Marina, she informs his version of the fall of Mexico. A brief examination of the historical texts which construct Marina will enhance our understanding of Dryden's portrait of the native woman.

Francisco Lopez de Gomara, Cortes's biographer and historian of the conquest of Mexico, and Bernal Diaz del Castillo, a soldier and eyewitness of the conquest, both emphasize the importance of Marina in the story of Cortes's conquest of Mexico. Diaz recounts Marina's story "[b]efore telling about the great Montezuma and his famous City of Mexico and the Mexicans";[9] her story precedes and therefore lays the foundation for the conquest of all New Spain: "without the help of Dona Marina we could not have understood the language of New Spain and Mexico," and with her help "things prospered with us."[10]

Diaz explains that Marina was secretly given to the Xicalango people by her parents, chiefs of the Caciques, so that her brother would succeed as heir to their chiefdom. After giving Marina away, they told their people that she had died. The Xicalango later gave Marina to the Tabascans.[11] After losing their battle with the Spaniards, the Tabascans gave Marina to Cortes as a peace offering, along with "bread, turkeys, fruits, and other provisions," as well as "four hundred pesos of gold, . . . and [nineteen other] female slaves to work for [the Spanish] army."[12] The presents, which Diaz cites as "things of little value, . . . [were] worth nothing in comparison with the twenty women that were given us, among them one very excellent woman called Dona Marina, for so she was named when she became a Christian."[13] Cortes gave one of these women, including Marina, to each of his captains. Later, during the decisive phase of his conquest, Marina became his lover and bore him a son; after the fall of Mexico, Cortes married her off to another conquistador.

Cortes recognized the value of Marina once he determined her ability as a translator. In Marina, Cortes saw the potential to subjugate the land and its peoples as well. She functioned as the voice through which Cortes spoke. According to Lopez, once Marina was established as Cortes's interpreter, he was able to put into effect his plan of conquest. Diaz repeatedly praises her for her ability to outwit each native group that Cortes encountered. Indeed, as Diaz states, she "proved herself such an excellent woman and good interpreter throughout the wars in New Spain, Tlaxcala and Mexico . . . Cortes always took her with him."[14] In one of his first "conquests," Diaz describes how Cortes took Marina with him to Caciques where she met with her family for the first time since her "death." Cortes brought Marina with him in order to impress upon her parents and brother the power of his authority; he knew the story of how Marina's parents had given her away, and he may have intended to use her miraculous "return" as a means to subdue the Caciques. Diaz states that when they assembled to hear Cortes's speech "about our holy religion, and about . . . [the Indian's] good treatment[,]"

[t]hese relations were in great fear of Dona Marina, for they thought that she had sent for them to put them to death, and they were weeping.

When Dona Marina saw them in tears, she consoled them and told them to have no fear, that when they had given her over to the men from Xicalango, they knew not what they were doing, and she forgave them for doing it, and she gave them many jewels of gold and raiment, and told them to return to their town, and said that God had been very gracious to her in freeing her from the worship of idols and making her a Christian, and letting her bear a son to her lord and master Cortes and in marrying her to such a gentleman as Juan Jaramillo, who was now her husband. That she would rather serve her husband and Cortes than anything else in the world, and would not exchange her place to be Cacica of all the provinces in New Spain.[15]

As in the English accounts of Pocahontas's conversion, Marina is empowered by her rejection of her own people in favor of the white men's religion and culture. According to Diaz, Marina was content to have been sold into slavery and cheated of her chiefdom; she sees her conversion as blessed and her service to the male Spaniards as a privilege and an honor. Diaz is drawing on a familiar narrative of Christian conversion to promote Spanish secular and economic power.

The description of the war in Cholula links Marina to the colonization of Mexico and, in particular, Montezuma's fall from power. Lopez writes that Montezuma directed Cortes to approach Mexico through Cholula, where he intended to launch a surprise attack on the white men. Marina discovered the plot from Cholulan priests, through "the manner she kn[ew] so well how to use,"[16] and from a Cholulan noblewoman who "liked the looks of the bearded men."[17] As a result of the information gathered by Marina, Cortes forestalled the attack, decimated the Cholulans, and greatly weakened Montezuma's plan to prevent the Spaniards' invasion of Mexico.

In Diaz's and Lopez's narratives, Marina repeatedly functions as a sexualized object of exchange between the white men and the natives, it is "the manner Marina knew so well how to use"—a "manner" that is both intellectual and sexual—that allows the Spanish exploitation and destruction of the Aztec people to succeed. Marina's story suggests, therefore, that conquest occurs over the native woman's body and through the conventions of the romance narrative. Because of the supposedly superior powers and irresistible attractiveness of the Spaniards, Marina and other women willingly give up their people and country to the colonizers. In effect, the native woman's desire is the ventriloquized desire of the white men: Marina becomes the fantasy figure who surrenders her desire to theirs. She is the first property Cortes acquires, a possession given to him as a "gift" (along with gold and silver) with other female slaves. Through Marina's mouth, ears, and womb, Cortes appropriates the New World. Yet, as Moraga points out, Marina is also constituted as evil— she betrays her own people to help the men she supposedly loves. Marina is therefore both heroine and evil woman, savior and betrayer.

To contextualize Dryden's account of Spanish colonization, I first shall examine William Davenant's *The Cruelty of the Spanish in Peru* (1658) and *The History of Sir Francis Drake* (1659),[18] which are crucial to the anti-Spanish drama of the mid to late seventeenth century and which, according to Dryden's California editors, greatly influenced his portrait of the conquest of Mexico.[19]

*Cruelty* and *Sir Francis Drake* were the only plays that Cromwell allowed to be performed during the Interregnum because they supported his anti-Spanish policies.[20] Davenant's portrayal of the Spanish and the Indians was in part influenced by John Phillips's translation of Las Casas's *The Tears of the Indians*. Las Casas's argument served the English as an excuse to project onto the Spanish their own guilt and anxieties about colonization. Following in the tradition of Las Casas and supporting Cromwell's Western Design,[21] then, Davenant's *Cruelty* and *Sir Francis Drake* attack the Spaniards' brutal methods of colonization and portray the English as virtuous colonists. As David Hoegberg points out, "Davenant's assault [on the Spanish] provides a veiling script that justifies English reconquest of the territory. . . . Davenant shows considerable sympathy for the Indians' sufferings at the hands of Spaniards. [Yet] he never lets that sympathy become a critique of colonialism itself."[22] The Spaniards, in Davenant's vision, are depicted as more uncivilized than the natives, while the English are presented as heroes who restore order and peace to the New World.

*Cruelty* begins by illustrating the "happy conditions" of the natives before the arrival of the Spanish, when the Indians were "govern'd by Nature" (I.i.1–3).[23] In their prelapsarian state, the natives declared they were free: "none for being strong did seek reward,/ Nor any for the space of Empire strove . . . / We fettr'd none, nor were by any bound;/None follow'd gold through the lab'rynths of the mine" (I.i.32–33,36–38). The natives lived "wildly" during this innocent golden age, without "right" and "claim, . . . none did riches wish;" they "lookt ever young,/And from restraints were free" (I.i.53,56,50–51). This was a time when "nakedness" was not a "shame" and when "none could want, and all were innocent" (I.i.69,71). However, the Indians' fall from innocence, though preordained to occur by the "sun's Chief Priest" with the arrival of the "bearded people . . . /Cruel men, idolators of gold," begins before the appearance of the Spaniards (II.i.7,5,8). The natives war among themselves, and this civil conflict leaves them weakened and susceptible to the Spanish. In this instance, Davenent, a royalist who loathed the rebellion against Charles I, may be displacing England's factionalism and civil unrest onto the Indians: their internal war invites and demands the force of an external ruler. The Indians are already fallen before the arrival of the Spanish "bearded men," and they therefore need to be converted, defeated, or killed by a greater moral and economic power. The arrival of the friendly colonist, the Englishman, is therefore posited as morally regenerative for the postlapsarian New World. By blaming the Spaniards for the cruelties that occur in the process of colonization, Davenant can make a de facto plea for the unification of Commonwealth and Royalist interests in the name of national self-interest and individual aggrandizement for merchants, investors, and adventurers.

In Davenant's play, as it will be in Dryden's subsequent works, it is the "fatal . . . passion" of the Indian ruler for a native woman which leads to the destruction of his people (*Cruelty*, III.i.1). The natives believe, "Our late great Inca fatally,/Did by a second wife/Eclipse his shining life . . . /Now rigid war is come and peace is gone" (III.i.32–34,42). For the Peruvians, the monarch's division of his "private bed" literally causes the division of his "public Empire" (III.i.11). Contrary to the tradition of his *"Royal Ancestors,"* the Inca does not marry his own sister, but chooses a daughter of an *"inferior Prince"* to be his second wife: *"[t]his foreign Beauty so far prevail'd on his passion, that she made him in his age assign a considerable part of his dominion to a younger son."* The younger son, *"growing ambitious after his father's death[,]"* attacked his older brother's lands. The Spanish land in Peru at the time of the war and make *"prodigious use of the division of the two brethren"* (83). In effect, the dangerous Indian woman is implicitly blamed for the disruption of patrilineal succession and the fall of the native empire.

When the natives first see the Spanish, they believe the strangers are gods. The Indians describe how the Spanish in "foreign shapes so strange appear,/ That wonderful they seem;/And strangeness breeds esteem:/And wonder engender fear;/And from our fear does adoration rise" (IV.i.25–29). The natives admire the Spanish because they fear them; this is no amicable relationship, then, but one predicated on submission, exploitation, and oppression. The natives' "adoration" soon turns to hatred when they are confined, tortured, and forced to dig for gold and silver. The Spaniards' methods of torture are particularly cruel; a native prince is roasted over a spit, while other natives are broken on racks (V.i). The Spanish "make the cramp, by waters drill'd, to cease/Men ready to expire, Baste them with drops of fire,/And then, they lay them on the rack for ease" (V.i.4–7). The natives point out, moreover, that while they are tortured supposedly on religious grounds, the Spaniards "will not permit/ We should our idols quit,/Because the Christian law makes converts free" (V.i.11–13). The conquistadors lose the veneer of religious justification for their atrocities. Davenant depicts the Spaniards as self-serving hypocrites who torment the Peruvians for profit alone; they need slaves and therefore do not convert the natives. The Spaniards also attack and torment "other Christians [Prostestants] landing here,/ . . . And those they so much worse than heathens deem,/ That they must tortur'd die./ The world still waste must lye,/Or else a prison be to all but them" (V.i.20,21–25). *Cruelty*, in other words, does not plead in defense of the natives' rights as much as it warns of the dangers the Spanish pose to the English. Davenant's attack on religious hypocrisy plays well with English anti-Catholicism.

Finally, in the last "Entry" of the play, the English arrive in Peru; and with their fictional appearance (the English did not, of course, invade Peru) the

Spaniards flee for their lives. The oppressed natives are now saved by the "English Lion" from "digging" the "dismal depths" of the "mines" (VI.I.29,24,13–14). In contrast to the cruelty of the Spaniards, the English will "rule as guests" (VI.i.42,47). Hoegberg points out that the description of the English colonizers as both rulers and guests mystifies the relationship of England to the New World: "Davenant wants us to believe that the English can have all the advantages of economic mastery bestowed by the colonial script and all the advantages of love and friendship."[24] The English command peacefully and amicably, and the natives are drawn to the English of their own accord. The play ends with the Peruvians and the English "salut[ing]" and "shak[ing] hands in sign of their future amity" (VI.i.48). The English are thus portrayed as humane colonizers—Christlike saviors—whom the natives welcome as their "guests," and to whom, presumably, the natives will willingly give gold. Davenant thus suggests that, for the English colonizers, riches are acquired without force or labour. Davenant also portrays a fantasy of the future in *Cruelty*: if the English succeed in ousting the Spanish from Peru, then England will acquire the gold which the Spanish are monopolizing.

In *Sir Francis Drake*, performed later that same season at the Cockpit, Davenant drew on Drake's first raid on the Spanish in the Caribbean in 1572–1573, in which escaped Spanish slaves (Moors) helped Drake capture a Spanish mule-train filled with treasures.[25] As in *Cruelty*, the Spanish are portrayed as evil colonizers from whom the heroic English save the oppressed Symerons and Indians. Though Drake's mariners are indeed interested in acquiring wealth—when the English sailors first spy land, one mariner cries, "The bowels of Peru/Shall be ript up and be our own" (I.i.33–34)—this is not the expedition's primary purpose.[26] Drake explains that the mariners' desire for gold is bound ideologically to a greater end: "That which enlightens, and does lead/The world, and all our vict'ries breed,/ We in those caverns shall behold,/ In seeing man's bright mistress, gold" (I.i.73–76). Davenant makes an imagistic connection between enlightening the natives and the brightness of a feminized gold. Unlike the Spanish, however, the English supposedly invade Peru not for profit but to attack their "country's foes" (I.i.68).

Like the Spanish men in Dryden's *Indian Emperour* (and Cortes in particular), who are figured as irresistible to Marina and other native women, Drake is presented by Davenant as a hero whom all non-European people admire and befriend. He is recognized instantly as a hero of the seas. When the king of the Symerons first meets Drake, he declares, "Welcome! and in my land be free,/And powerful as thou art at sea" (II.i.75–76), and he vows to help the English in their battle against the Spanish. Drake, in his turn, admires the world to which he has been welcomed. He observes how "Their dwelling seems so fresh and flourishing,/As if it still the nurs'ry were/Of all the seeds that furnish out the spring/For every clime, and all the year." The New World is contrasted to the Old: "Here, nature to her summer court retires:/Our northern region is the shade,/Where she grows cold, and looks decay'd,/And seems to sit by artificial fires" (III.i.37–41). Drake's observations resemble those of a lover admiring a woman he wishes to possess; nature in the New World is virginal, abundant, and alive. The English are figured as lovers: "When embrac'd by his friends:/ Then [Drake] is calm and gentle made,/As love's soft whispers in a shade" (III.i.78–80). Yet Drake is a "calm and gentle" friend and lover to the others only when they "embrace" him. He protects the feminized Symerons and Indians from their Spanish oppressors on the condition that they fully submit to him.

While the English army marches toward the Spanish, however, Captain Rouse informs Drake that the Symerons have acted blasphemously by interrupting a Spanish wedding feast and stealing the bride. The Symerons consider this act retaliation against "the cruelties which they/Have often felt beneath the Spaniards' sway,/Who midst the triumphs of our nuptial feasts/Have forc'd our brides, and slaughter'd all our guests./ . . . Revenge does all the fetters break of law" (V.i.155–159,161). But, for Drake, the abduction of a white woman is a heinous crime—particularly since the abductors are Moors. The Moors consequently must be reduced to the overdetermined role of black male sexual predators who threaten the purity of European women and, therefore, the purity of the white race. The Moors thus become, in Frantz Fanon's words regarding black male masculinity in a colonial context, "eclipsed" and "turned into penis[es]."[27] When Drake discovers "a beautiful lady tied to a tree, adorn'd with the ornaments of a Bride, with her hair dishevel'd, and complaining, with her hand towards Heaven . . . [, and] About her are discerned the Symerons who took her prisoner" (68), he is angered and appalled. He vows to fight the Symerons for their crime of potential interracial sex, crying "Arm! Arm! the honour of my nation/turns." For Drake, whatever crimes the Spaniards have committed, the "gentle sex must still be free" (V.i.107,165). The Symerons are quickly subdued, and the Spanish bride is liberated.

In this scene, then, the Symerons demonstrate their need to be civilized by the English colonizers because the conquistadors have succeeded only in teaching the Moors to act barbarically. Just as Prospero's justification for his control of Caliban hinges on the native's attack on Miranda's "honor," so too the Moors' abduction of a white woman establishes Drake's absolute right to attack the Symerons. His treatment of women, in this respect, supposedly distinguishes him from both Spaniard and Symeron; both exploit women in their battles as they do material goods. In contrast, Drake supposedly views the desire for women as he views the obsession for gold and silver. These "treasures" are not the purpose of his battle—he claims to scorn such base motivations in favor of saving the New World from chaos and savagery. However, in saving the New World, Drake simultaneously acquires all that he supposedly scorns—women, gold, land, and slaves—on seemingly just and morally defensible grounds.

After Drake frees the Spanish bride, however, the English continue to pursue their European adversaries. When Drake, Rouse, and their men come upon a Spanish Reco (mule train) laden with silver and gold from the mines, Drake claims to:

> despise
> That treasure which I now would make your [English] prize:
> Unworthy 'tis to be your chiefest aim,
> For this attempt is not for gold, but fame;
> Which is not got when we the Reco get,
> But by subduing those who rescue it.
> (VI.i.22–27)

Drake does not wish to be remembered for the wealth he acquired in this battle but for "subduing" the Spaniards. For Davenant, Drake represents an ethos of honor. When the Spanish flee, and the English win the battle (and their Recoes) Drake states:

> Those who hereafter our legend look,
> And value us by that which we have took,
>     May over-reckon it, and us misprize . . .
> Your glory, valiant English, must be known,
>     When men shall read how you did dare
>     To sail so long, and march so far,
> To tempt a strength much greater than your own.
> (VI.i.116–118,124–127)

As these lines suggest, Drake repeatedly claims that the purpose of his battle is to assert England's military power, and achieve glory and fame. Davenant casts Drake in an epic mold so that English piracy appears in "heroic" terms, veiling the aggressive and imperialistic ideology of the seventeenth-century English expanionism. In Davenant's portrayal, the English, unlike the Spanish, are selfless heroes who fight for greater purposes than the acquisition of gold and silver. Their greater purpose—English expansion—is figured as mutually beneficial for the English and the non-Europeans. The play ends with a description of a "Grand Dance . . . consisting of [English mariners and soldiers,] two Symerons, and a Peruvian; intimating, by their several interchange of salutations, their mutual desires of amity" (76). Davenant therefore posits English colonization as the forging of a friendship between England and the New World and as a means to promote an ideology of national and colonial unity that mystifies British overseas exploitation.

While Dryden was influenced by *Cruelty* and *Drake, The Indian Queen* and *Indian Emperour* were written during a very different political climate—the early years of the Restoration—and his version of Spanish colonization differs somewhat from Davenant's. In Dryden's plays the Spanish and the English are not pitted against one another; instead, English politics are symbolically grafted onto the Spanish and native wars. Max Harris notes that both Spaniard and native are constructed ambivalently in Dryden's plays, and though "different" they are presented "faintly" on equal terms.[28] He suggests that Dryden attempts to minimize the differences between the two cultures in order to heighten the "matters of contemporary debate" and de-emphasize the "historical setting."[29] Dryden's and Howard's *Indian Queen* and Dryden's *Indian Emperour*, written soon after Charles II's restoration, use the history of the Spanish conquest of Mexico to promote a royalist ideology "and to explore the nature of imperial power and cultural difference." While the Spanish conquistadors as a group are by no means portrayed as perfect heroes, Cortes, their leader, represents an ideal ruler who stabilizes the disordered native society, subjects it to the civilizing influence of Christianity, and overcomes the greed and villainy of some of the Spanish conquistadors. Bridget Orr argues, "*The Indian Emperour* is carefully structured to set religious and legal grounds for Spanish rule in the Indies against the desire for plunder, pleasure and glory."[30]

Dryden's positive treatment of Cortes may be the result of Charles II's relationship with Spain. Although Spain remained England's competitor during the Restoration, the formerly exiled royalists had positive relations with Spain during the Interregnum. John Loftis points out that

[i]t would be difficult to overestimate the importance of the exile in determining the Spanish vogue in Restoration drama, a vogue that was a Royalist phenomenon, a dramatic expression of tastes the Cavaliers acquired or had reinforced in their wanderings in Spain. . . . Charles was surrounded by men who knew Spanish or had spent extended periods in Spain.[31]

During the period that Cromwell attacked Spanish Hispaniola, Spain became "receptive to overtures from Charles . . . [and they] entered into negotiations with him."[32] As a result, Charles and his followers spent four years in the Spanish Netherlands. In 1659, the last year of his exile, Charles travelled throughout Spain. Charles's and his courtiers' familiarity with Spanish language, literature, and culture, as well as their Catholic leanings, may have encouraged Dryden to soften the anti-Spanish sentiment in his version of the Spanish conquest of Peru.

But perhaps more importantly, Dryden may have chosen to examine colonial expansion in a Spanish and Mexican context because it allowed him to explore the complexities of miscegenation and the desire for the Indian woman in an unthreatening way. In *The Indian Emperour*, in contrast to every other English play in the seventeenth century that I am aware of, miscegenation takes place successfully. Indeed, the play ends with the fictional conclusion of Cortes marrying Cydaria, Montezuma's daughter. Thus Dryden examines an already lost ideal in the English colonies—the memory of John Rolfe and Pocahontas—and he draws on Spanish methods of assimilation and acculturation to play out the fantasy and desire for the dangerous native woman: "the longing for what they [the English] fear."[33]

For Dryden, then, the story of the Spanish conquest functions, at least in part, as a royalist allegory of Charles II's restoration, yet he significantly marks the monarchical restoration in racialized and gendered terms. In *Astraea Redux*, for example, Dryden suggests that Charles II's "banishment" (79) during the Interregnum turned the ordered social structure of England upside down: "The rabble now such freedom did enjoy/ As winds at sea that use it to destroy/Blind as the Cyclops, and as wild as he,/ They owned a lawless savage liberty" (43–46).[34] In effect, without royal rule, the people of England go native. Charles II's restoration brings the English world to "times whiter series," the

> nation, with united interest blest,
> Not now content to poise, shall sway the rest.
> Abroad [the English] empire shall no limits know . . .
> [The King's] much loved fleet shall with a wide command
> Besiege the petty monarchs of the land; . . .
> At home the hateful names and parties cease
> And factious souls are wearied into peace . . .
> Oh happy age! Oh times like those alone
> By fate reserved for great Augustus' throne!
> When the joint growth of arms and arts foreshew
> The world a monarch, and that monarch you.
> (292, 296–298, 300–301, 312–313, 320–323)

The king's exertion of international military force brings an end to England's factionalism. Foreign adventure is depicted as a means to overcome internal divisions at home and secure an unprecedented and cleansed English prosperity.

Que [vira]. *By their protection let us beg to live;*
*They came here not to Conquer, but Forgive.*

(Prologue, 1–20)

This prelapsarian scene foreshadows the colonization of the New World in *The Indian Emperour*. In the Prologue, the New World is a Golden Age land of temperate climate, free of war and avarice. The natives live in harmony with nature. But the loud noises which foretell of the Spaniard's invasion give them alarm, and their sleep ends. Both the boy and girl look upon the imminent invasion of the Spaniards as inevitable and even explicitly redemptive. Quevira paradoxically suggests that although they are in Eden, the natives need to be forgiven. For Dryden, the forgiveness which the natives require is Christian redemption; thus the Prologue ends on a note which indicates a yearning for the arrival of the Christlike white man. Like Marina, who is happier once she is converted to Christianity, these natives look forward to being saved. While the natives in the Prologue live peacefully, the Indian world within the two plays is already fallen, already at war. What the Indians of the Golden Age are lacking is the spiritual salvation promised by their Christian conquerors.

The Prologue is (dis)placed before *The Indian Queen*—a play about conquest and usurpation. This war is only among Indians themselves, as the Europeans do not arrive until the sequel, *The Indian Emperour*. By situating the Prologue directly before *The Indian Queen*, Dryden identifies the reason for the fall of Mexico as being the fault not of conquering Europeans, but of the wild and unruly natives who lack the means of salvation. *The Indian Queen* dramatizes the fictional battle between the Ynca King and the Mexican Queen Zempoalla. Zempoalla is an evil and rebellious usurper; Montezuma describes her as the woman "to whom all grief is due" (V.i.300). She has killed her brother and stolen his throne, exiling his wife, Amexia, and their infant, Montezuma, into the wilderness. Montezuma is "bred . . . in a Cave" unaware of his true royal lineage—"the mighty secret [kept] from [his] ear,/ Lest heat of blood to some strange course shou'd steer" him (V.i.237–239). As the play opens, a battle between Queen Zempoalla and the Ynca has just ended, and the Peruvians have conquered Mexico, thanks to Montezuma. As a reward, the king offers him a "Kingdom . . . where [he] will Reign" (I.i.29); yet Montezuma says that he

beg[s] not Empires, those my Sword can gain;
But for my past and future Service too,
What I have done, and what I mean to do;

For this of *Mexico* which I have won,
And Kingdoms I will Conquer yet unknown;
I only ask from fair *Orazia*'s Eyes
To reap the Fruits of all my Victories.

(I.i.30–36)

Instead of land, Montezuma requests the Ynca's daughter Orazia. Yet the Ynca king will not give up his daughter to this "Young Man of unknown Race" (I.i.38). In this instance, Dryden casts "race" in the same terms as class; Montezuma is not equal to Orazia or her father because his lineage is not known. Consequently, Montezuma's desire for Orazia is perceived by the Peruvian king as akin to rebellion, as a brazen attempt to "mix . . . base" and royal "blood" (I.i.50). Not surprisingly, the Ynca is so angered by Montezuma's request that he binds the young man in chains and intends to kill him. Restoration audiences would certainly perceive the ideologically loaded nature of Montezuma's transgressive demand in this context. Yet the scene creates conflicting responses because the audience knows that Montezuma is himself the legitimate royal heir. Dryden's and Howard's *Indian Queen* sets up a very traditional sort of dilemma in love and honor plays, where there are two competing claims to honor.

Thus begins the battle which continues throughout *The Indian Queen* and *The Indian Emperour*: the patrilineal fight for royal power is enacted symbolically as a fight over the female body. Male ownership and control of the royal native woman are equated with absolute and divine power. In addition to the Ynca's refusal in *The Indian Queen* to give up his daughter to Montezuma, the two potential heirs to the Mexican throne also vie for the same woman: Acasis, Zempoalla's son, and Montezuma, the true king, both love Orazia. Their political fight is cast in terms of their passion for Orazia. Montezuma exclaims, "Oh Tyrant Love, how cruel are thy Laws!/ I forfeit Friendship, or betray thy Cause," to which Acasis responds, "Our Lives we to each others Friendships owe;/But Love calls back what Friendship did bestow:/Love has its Cruelties, but Friendship none;/And now we fight in Quarrels not our own" (IV.ii.37–38,41–44). Politics are projected onto love. When Orazia declares that she loves Montezuma, Acasis decides to commit suicide—providing an easy solution for homosocial rivalry—and Montezuma's competitor for the Mexican throne is thus eliminated because the king has won Orazia's love. The possession of Orazia is therefore equated with imperial power, and the qualities of heroism and leadership are made manifest in an idealized love.

This device, in which the acquisition of a royal native woman represents the appropriation of political power, is restaged throughout both plays. In *The Indian Queen*, it is symbolic of the battle between competing nations—Peru and Mexico—as well as of the restoration of royal authority, while in *The Indian Emperour*, the battle over the native woman is symbolic of the war between the Old World and the New. Immediately after conquering Mexico for the Peruvian Ynca, Montezuma demands Orazia—a demand which leads ultimately to his restoration as emperor of Mexico; and it will be because of his love for a native woman that he will lose Mexico to the Spaniards in *The Indian Emperour*. In both of these plays, love becomes the means to mystify the horrors of conquest.

In conquering Mexico, Montezuma overcomes the powerful, dangerous, and rebellious Zempoalla, who usurped the crown of Mexico from Montezuma's father and mother, and took a lover, Traxalla. Zempoalla loses her mind (and power) when she falls in love with Montezuma, her nephew. The name "Traxalla" is taken by Dryden and Howard from Spanish accounts of the Tlaxcallan rebels, whom Cortes befriended in order to fight Montezuma, and they were crucial to the Spaniards' victory. Zempoalla's love for Traxalla emphasizes her role as a rebel and usurper, allowing Dryden and Howard to make her responsible for the destruction of Mexico. Zempoalla recalls, for Royalists, the horrors of English rebellion in the 1640s, when Charles I was decapitated. For the dramatists, therefore, the native queen is linked symbolically to political unrest in England; Zempoalla represents the divisive forces that need to be vanquished in order to reaffirm royal authority both in Mexico and in England.

Montezuma's return is therefore connected symbolically to the restoration of Charles II; he is the legitimate king who returns from exile to reclaim his throne and restore order to a kingdom in chaos. With his restoration, peace between the Peruvians and Mexicans is established, and Zempoalla commits suicide. The forces of evil will their own demise. When the Ynca king discovers that Montezuma is the lawful heir to Mexico's crown, he sanctions the union with Orazia. Montezuma thus ascends to the throne in the same moment that he acquires his wife and subdues the dangerous native queen: "Deaths fatal triumphs joyn'd with those of love./Love crowns the dead, and death Crowns him that lives,/ Each gains the Conquest the other gives" (V.i.308–310). In other words, the repression of the native woman "crowns" the true king: Montezuma's "conquest" is both of woman and a throne. This dynamic also works to identify the legitimate Montezuma with the restoration of Charles II. Just as the native women were taken into captivity by the Spaniards, baptized, and made their lovers, slaves, and translators, so too Zempoalla is replaced and erased by the new queen of Mexico, Orazia—the subdued and submissive royal native woman. However, as we shall see in *The Indian Emperour*, Zempoalla, and all that she represents, cannot be entirely destroyed.

In the first scene of *The Indian Emperour*, the Spaniards describe the New World as a feminized, fertile, and virginal land. By now, of course, this is a very familiar refrain—part of the ongoing effort to interest the upper classes in investing in plantations in the New World.

> Cort[es]. Here nature spreads her fruitful sweetness round,
> Breaths on the Air and broods upon the ground.
> Here days and nights the only seasons be,
> The Sun no Climat does so gladly see . . .
> Vasq[uez]. Methinks we walk in dreams on fairy Land,
> Where golden Ore lies mixt with common sand;
> Each downfal of a flood the Mountains pour,
> From their rich bowels rolls a silver shower.
> Cort[es]. Heaven from all ages wisely did provide
> This wealth, and for the bravest Nation hide,
> Who with four hundred foot, and forty horse,
> Dare boldy go a New found World to force.
>
> (I.i.21–24; 27–34)[37]

For Cortes and Vasquez, the Edenic New World offers infinite material wealth. The Spaniards conflate theology with military might and with the desire for the wealth of the natives' land. According to Cortes, God has provided this abundant land for the Spanish to acquire because of their innate superiority and power. It is theirs for the taking.

The marriage scene which immediately follows takes place in Mexico among the royal Indians—Montezuma, his children, Cydaria, Odmar, and Guyomar, and Zempoalla's children, Orbellan, Alibech, and Almeria. The marriage scene highlights the relationship in Dryden's vision among the native women, the land, and mineral wealth. Just as the land and gold described by the Spaniards whet the spectators' anticipation for the coming conquest, the marriageable native women are displayed as objects to be possessed. Orazia has died before the play opens, and Montezuma announces his plan to choose a second wife, Almeria, the vengeful daughter of Zempoalla. He is blinded to her desire for revenge by his fatal passion for her: she hates the king for taking the throne from her mother and father and declares early in the play that she intends to destroy him. By falling in love, Montezuma, the Europeanized hero of *The Indian Queen*, has, in the first act, already lost his virility and power. Love, which is figured as a metaphor for conquest in *The Indian Queen*, now becomes the cause of Montezuma's downfall. In Fray Benardino de Sahagun's historical account, Montezuma is portrayed as weak—afraid of Cortes because he believes the Spaniard is "Quetzacoatl," the white God.[38] Dryden deflects Montezuma's weakness onto his love for a woman. His misguided desire for Almeria and Guyomar's and Odmar's similarly misguided love for Alibech lead to the fall of the Mexican Empire.

Man's rational nature is thus destroyed in the Mexican kingdom by his passion for the native woman. Montezuma is presented as a man of European reason—he argues cleverly with the Spanish to frustrate their desires to impose Christian doctrine and Spanish law and to acquire wealth. Montezuma says he respects the white God, but prefers his own for religion "must be in Men, not Lands" (I.ii.298), and states he will not "in a base subjection live" (I.i.325). As a generous man, however, Montezuma relinquishes all his "Gold," because the natives have no need for it other than their "heathenous" religious uses (I.ii.278). It is all the more striking, then, that this Europeanized, peace-loving nobleman should be destroyed by his passion. Dryden establishes that love makes Montezuma a misguided and tragically doomed ruler, who goes to the high priest in the magician's cave not to find out "th'event of doubtful war" (II.i.2) but "to know *Almeria*'s mind" (II.i.7). After the native priest invokes a spirit who warns of Montezuma's possible downfall, the Indian emperor shouts, "But of my Crown thou too much care do'st take,/That which I value more, my Love's at stake" (II.i.65–66). The king's honor and power, according to Dryden, are supposedly destroyed because of his love for a woman, not because of the political crises provoked by the arrival of the Spanish.

Love also leads to civil war within and the destruction of the native royal family: Montezuma's sons become rivals for Alibech. Although Guyomar upholds his duty as a son and prince to his father the king, Odmar is led by his passion to usurp his father's authority and destroy his country. In the nuptial ceremony in act 1, the two brothers must choose their wives. But there is, as far as we know, only one princess for them to choose, since their father will marry Almeria and Cydaria is their sister. Consequently, they fight over Alibech throughout the course of the play. But the fight is presented in terms that suggest Alibech has led them to this battle; she refuses to tell them which one she loves and sets up a test of allegiance to gauge who will win her hand(II.ii.87–99). The princess clearly sees herself as property: she offers herself as the prize to be won by the brother who is most dutiful to his country. Despite her protest in favor of "duty to country" over personal pleasure, Odmar believes Alibech will love him if he is most faithful to her, while Guyomar, the noble one, tries to save Mexico and repeatedly stands by his father. For John Winterbottom, Guyomar is the true "vessel of honor and virtue" in the play. Yet, ironically, at the end of the play, Guyomar's honor leads him to relinquish completely his right to Mexico; he refuses to share his throne with Cortes, and in act 5, he departs on supposedly valorous grounds.

This "honorable" departure obscures the history of colonization by depicting the natives' submission to the Spaniards as entirely self-imposed. Guyomar and Alibech voluntarily retreat to a Northern barren land—free of gold and minerals and, hence, free of conquering Spaniards.

In Dryden's portrait of the Spanish Conquest, then, "*Indians* joyn the *Indians* to subdue" (I.i.36); the native princes are responsible for their own losses because of their passion for an irresistible woman. Not only is Alibech presented as the object of the brothers' battle, just as Cydaria is depicted as the object over whom the Europeans and natives war, but the native woman is presented as inviting this fatal bodily desire; she is the chaos within the native culture which cannot be controlled—at least by Indians. Alibech alters her demand of the brothers in act 4, scene 2, when she believes her family and country will die if they do not submit to the Spaniards; she asks that the princes go against Montezuma's command to fight for their freedom and instead "save" their people from "certain death" (IV.ii.36). She suggests to Guyomar that, "While *Montezuma* sleeps, call in the Foe:/The Captive General your design may know:/His Noble heart, to Honour ever true,/Knows how to spare as well as to subdue" (IV.ii.46–49). In effect, like Marina, Alibech betrays her country and king; she incites rebellion and civil misrule in the name of the greater good of European conquest. Like Quevira in the Prologue of *The Indian Queen*, she now believes that the Spaniards are benevolent gods who will save the natives. When Guyomar asks Alibech why she has changed her mind, she states, "When Kings grow stubborn, slothful, or unwise,/Each private man for publick good should rise" (IV.ii.74–75). In this instance, Alibech reproduces the logic of the English Commonwealthsmen of the 1640s and 1650s. Guyomar warns her against such rebellion: "Take heed, Fair Maid, how Monarchs you accuse:/ Such reasons none but impious Rebels use:/ . . . Kings by free consent their Kingdoms take,/Strict as those Sacred Ties which Nuptials make" (IV.ii.76–77,80–81). Alibech is presented as an untrustworthy royal subject; she vacillates in her allegiance from Montezuma to Cortes and tries to convince Montezuma's sons to follow her rebellious will. Like her mother Zempoalla and sister Almeria, Alibech represents the political rebel who needs to be dominated by a powerful Christian conqueror.

Despite Alibech's new "test," Guyomar remains true to his father and country. But, after he successfully captures Vasquez, Pizarro, and their men, Alibech changes her allegiance once again: "I gave my Love to the most brave in War;/But that the King must Judge" (IV.iii.35–36). Alibech turns to Montezuma to decide whom she will marry, and because Guyomar has remained true to his father and king—his decision is both personal and political— Montezuma declares that Guyomar shall marry her. In the next scene, Odmar avenges his lost love by literally "Sink[ing]" his "Empire," "Father" and

"Brother" (IV.iii.61), releasing the captured Spaniards in exchange for Alibech. Vasquez agrees to the bargain, but he insists that he will also win a native woman whose name he does not know. After Odmar and the Spaniards win the ensuing battle, Odmar discovers that the woman whom Vasquez desires is Alibech. In Dryden's vision, then, Alibech functions as a sign for Mexico— its wealth, its culture, its desirability, its dangers. Like Diaz and Lopez, Dryden obscures the cost of the colonial project to the Mexican people by framing the tale of conquest as the trafficking in women or as unreasonable desires for the native woman—which seems to be equated with the greed of the Spanish priest.

The figure of Alibech as the desirable and yet disorderly woman who leads the princes into destruction not only mystifies the economic purpose of colonization by portraying her elimination as necessary for the Indian people but reifies the misogynistic view of woman as barbarous and the nationalistic view of non-Europeans as "untaught . . . salvage[s]" in need of redemption (I.i.10). Alibech causes the destruction of both brothers (one loses his nation, the other his life); therefore, from the European point of view, she needs to be expelled from Mexico. For Dryden, Alibech's supposedly willing departure from Mexico in act 5 symbolizes the surrender of all of the Indian people and their natural resources to the European conquerors. At the very end of the play, when Cortes wins the battle with the Indians and offers to let Guyomar jointly rule the county with him, the Indian prince believes it would be beneath his honor to do so. He chooses, instead, to go North with Alibech to a postlapsarian barren land "Where Rocks lye cover'd with Eternal Snow;/Thin Herbage in the Plains, and Fruitless Fields,/The Sand no Gold, the Mine no Silver yields" (V.ii.369–371). The exile of the noble, rational, and sovereign Guyomar and the dangerous Alibech leaves the abundant natural resources of the New World in the hands of the purportedly noble and regenerative European, Cortes. In Dryden's fantasy, the New World is won by the Europeans by heavenly right. The fallen Indians leave Eden because of a divine edict that leaves the riches of South America for the Spaniards.

While Montezuma and his sons are unable to resist the chaotic forces of passion, Cortes is depicted as a man who rises above the Hobbesian chaos in which the others are mired; he is self-controlled and therefore possesses the honorable skills with which to subdue the wild native woman and the New World. Cortes is untouchable. Almeria cannot kill him—she becomes attracted to him like the Cholulan woman who betrays her people because of the Spaniard's good looks—nor can Montezuma. Characterized by self-regulation, the Spanish conquistador is never overpowered by emotion. For example, when the "burning" and "disorder'd" Almeria offers herself along with "the Crown of *Mexico*" to Cortes (IV.i.67,73,63), he coolly refuses her:

In wishing nothing we enjoy still most;
For even our wish is in possession lost:
Restless we wander to a new desire,
And burn our selves by blowing up the Fire:
We toss and turn about our Feaverish will,
When all our ease must come by lying still:
For all the happiness Mankind can gain
Is not in pleasure, but in rest from pain.

(IV.i.107–114)

Cortes is figured as a Christian stoic, or a man of Foucauldian self-policing and self-restraint: he never lets himself grow "feaverish" with passion or sexual desire, nor is he seduced by the promise of power. Cortes pledges his love to Cydaria and remains true to her. Even his love for Cydaria does not destroy him; she is merely part of his colonial plan. He does not fight for gold or power like the greedy Vasquez, Pizarro, and Christian priest. Again and again, he restrains the Spanish attack on Montezuma's empire. He is shocked when he discovers that the Christian priest has tortured Montezuma in order to baptize the king and discover where the Mexican gold is hidden. In response to seeing Montezuma tortured on the rack, he cries, "What dismal sight is this, which takes from me/ All the delight that waits on Victory!" (V.ii.113–114). Cortes sees the desire for gold as the "Accursed" force which causes the Spaniards to commit horrific "crimes" (V.ii.135), and he is elevated above the greedy conquistadors. The noble Cortes does not attack the Indian Orbellan (Zempoalla's son) after he discovers the prince had meant to kill him in his sleep. Instead, he kills Orbellan only in self-defense, when the Indian prince leads a duplicitous attack against the Spanish. Yet, in killing Orbellan, who betrays his emperor and country to win Cydaria back from Cortes, the Spaniard rids the native culture of a purportedly evil political rebel. Cortes also restrains and admonishes the Taxallans for attacking the Mexicans in act 1, even though they have been successful. Unlike Vasquez, who accepts a bribe for his freedom, Cortes will not bargain with the natives for his.

Cortes thus wins his reward of the native woman and her land precisely because he lacks desire. Cortes is always and already in the New Paradise: he is the civilized, rational, self-controlled European man who is at home in the idealized Golden Age of the New World. The man of the New Paradise is, then, characterized by self-containment. Unlike the native men and women such as Montezuma, Almeria, Odmar, and Zempoalla, who have fallen prey to their "Feaverish will" and desire for bodily "pleasure" (IV.i.111,114), Cortes rationally exercises self-control. Ironically, he resembles the "boy" and "girl" of the Prologue of *The Indian Queen* more than the natives themselves do. He does not desire the "use of the natural world" or its "possession," nor does he look to fight or "quarrel." Though the Spaniard loves Cydaria and invades the kingdom to win her, it is ultimately the Indians who are depicted as betraying and defeating themselves.

Cortes's rational qualities are presented, therefore, as redemptive for both the New World and for the Old. Given the symbolically feminized chaos Cortes finds when he arrives in the Mexican kingdom, his conquest is portrayed by Dryden as inevitable and morally regenerative. Not only does his behavior contrast sharply to the stereotypes of the cruel and greedy Pizarro and Vasquez, but he surpasses Montezuma in his ability to control his desires and passions. Cortes thus fulfills Quevira's wish in the Prologue: he offers the Indians both "protection" (from their disorderly and factionalized selves) and Christian "forgiveness" (for their sins). Cydaria, the only noblewoman who is not a daughter of the evil Zempoalla, is drawn to the white God. Because there is no available native nobleman for Cydaria to marry—other than Orbellan, the evil son of Zempoalla—the entrance of "Heavenly" Cortes appears to be, as Quevira predicts, providential (I.ii.235). The white hero will save the pure Cydaria, who is the "only space bewtixt the Clouds" (II.ii.12) of the wars in Mexico, and thereby prevent the destruction of the royal line. Cortes is immediately drawn to Cydaria, whose "beauty" he "gaze[s upon] till [he is] blind" (I.ii.352), and Cydaria cannot resist his "Honour which does Love controul" (II.ii.38) and his "power of Life and Death" (II.ii.16).

Properly submissive and willing to relinquish her own cultural identity, like the historical Cortes's translator, Dona Marina, and royal, like Pocahontas, Cydaria is posited as the ideal wife, subject, and property for the Christian legislator. She contrasts sharply to Alibech and Almeria, who cannot be absolutely tamed. Indeed, Cydaria is depicted as inciting her people's attacker. She is always pleased when Cortes conquers, approves of the death of Orbellan, does not express remorse when her father dies or her city is destroyed, but instead begs to remain by Cortes's side throughout the play. A pristine version of the classic betrayer of the Mexican natives—La Malinche, Malintzin, or Dona Marina  Cydaria is "La Chingada." She is representative of the external and internal wilderness which needs and wants to be invaded—the bowels of the (female) earth which willingly forego their treasures for the imperial project.

Yet, it must be remembered, in the 1660s all of these Malinche surrogates—Zempoalla, Almeria, Alibech, and Cydaria—are played by white women pretending to be Indian women (in white face and English costume), and the Spaniards are English men playing conquistadors. Here the acting out of miscegenation and the longing for the darker woman of the New World are undermined by the performance itself, which can never be a true replica of that which is lost. Once again, as we have seen throughout this work, English nationhood and English colonialism rely on the erasure of Indian peoples and cultures, not on assimilation and acculturation through intermarriage. But the playing of Indian women, nonetheless, reflects the ambivalent and disturbing bond between English women and Indian women, and the (feared) potential for the blurring of English self and racial other in the performance of inter-cultural colonial exchange.

# FOUR

# Aphra Behn's *The Widow Ranter*

[T]he Plantations, which are farther remov'ed from . . . [the]
Royal Presence, have those kindly Beams more weakly reflected on them. Their distance makes 'em liable to be ill used
by Men, that over-act Her Sacred Authority, and under-act
Her Vertues.

Robert Beverley
*The History and Present State of Virginia*, 1705

I began this study with Shakespeare's *The Tempest*, quite possibly the most
pivotal literary text in critical studies of colonial discourse in the early modern period. This chapter comes full circle, then, in that I conclude by examining Aphra Behn's dramatization of colonization. I would argue that just
as *The Tempest* functions as a central text in Renaissance colonial discourse,
so too Behn's *Oroonoko* and *Widow Ranter* operate as crucial points of analysis for race and gender studies of the Restoration and early eighteenth century. Ever growing numbers of critics examine the novel, and many in-
expensive versions of the work are available to the public.[1] *Oroonoko* has
entered the canon with a vengeance. Indeed, as Srivinas Aravamudan
writes, "recent critical attention [to *Oroonoko*] borders on the obsessional."[2]
While the novel is immensely popular, Behn's important colonial play has
been comparatively overlooked. With the exception of two fine recent essays on *The Widow Ranter* by Margaret Ferguson and Margo Hendricks, and
brief discussions of the play by Joseph Roach, Jacqueline Pearson, and Janet
Todd, the play has gone unnoticed.[3] In this chapter, I will look closely at
Behn's *Widow Ranter* (ca.1688–1689), and I will point to crucial aspects of
*Oroonoko* (1688) which surface in the play. Before examining *The Widow
Ranter*, however, I will situate the play in the context of the history of Bacon's Rebellion in Virginia, and the Exclusion Crisis and fall of the Stuart
throne in 1688. In doing so, I will demonstrate that Behn's play discloses the
ambiguities and tensions of the colonial project in Virginia, as well as the

enormity of the cost of expansionism to Native Americans. In addition, I will show how Behn's depiction of women differs from the male playwrights in this study. The complex interrelationship of white women and native women, and the oppression of women in general in a colonial context, are questioned in *The Widow Ranter*.

In contrast to Dryden's portrait of a heroic colonial enterprise in his *Indian Emperour* and *Indian Queen* (displaced to a distant time period and to Spanish colonial territories), *The Widow Ranter* is far less optimistic about English colonial nationhood or divine royal power. This difference can (in part) be accounted for in the change in the political climate during the two decade gap between Dryden's and Behn's plays; Dryden wrote his *Indian Queen* and *Indian Emperour* at the onset of Charles II's restoration to the throne, while Behn wrote during the demise of James II's reign. Further, as Bridget Orr points out, after 1680 the focus shifted in the drama, "from a critical representation of Spanish or Oriental empire, to the emergent mercantile imperium governed by William and Mary. Here, finally, the new model empire was sometimes itself the subject."[4] In effect, in *The Widow Ranter*, Behn turns away from the genre of the Oriental or Spanish colonial drama which was popular during the first twenty years of the Restoration, to a more immediate political tragicomedy composed of a generic blend of anti-Puritan comedy and love and honor tragedy. Perhaps, also, because of England's prosperity in Virginia by the late seventeenth century, Behn does not need to displace her version of interracial romance onto other European nations as did her male playwright predecessors, but she demonstrates how the Virginia colonists are in great sociopolitical conflict nonetheless. More importantly, as Orr also suggests, Behn's heroic native protagonists in the *The Widow Ranter* (and African and native protagonists in *Oroonoko*) become "victims of a state governed by trade."[5] I would argue further that in *The Widow Ranter*, Behn's native *woman*, in particular, is depicted as a victim of the sociopolitical conflicts within the Virginia colony and of the mercantilist economy of English colonial expansionism.

Ferguson's essay, "News From the New World: Miscegenous Romance in Aphra Behn's *Oroonoko* and *The Widow Ranter*," links Behn's deviant status as a woman writer[6] to the characters of Nathaniel Bacon in *The Widow Ranter* and Oroonoko in *Oroonoko*,[7] and suggests that Behn competes with and thus effaces both black and Indian female heroines: Nathaniel Bacon's love, Semernia, the Indian queen, and Oroonoko's wife, Imoinda.[8] Hendricks, in "Civility, Barbarism, and Aphra Behn's *The Widow Ranter*," argues miscegenation must be halted in the play, because it registers the dangers of blurring races and the potential of assimilating Indians into English culture.[9] Hendricks concludes that "race" in *The Widow Ranter* is used to consolidate and unify English civility.[10] Roach argues rightly that the play is about the fear of interracial contact and "of future generations threatening to be born."[11] While it may be true that Behn participates in and reproduces a colonial discourse which promotes imperial expansion (especially in *Oroonoko*), as Ferguson and Hendricks propose, the tragic aspects of the imperial project are registered quite forcefully—and given Behn's knowledge of the historical accounts—accurately, in the deaths of both Semernia and Imoinda, and in the problematic of interracial desire. Ferguson and Hendricks fail to assess fully, moreover, how Behn's colonial vision fits in with the larger historical questions regarding the symbolism of the woman-as-land metaphor in the seventeenth century, as well as with the complexities of playing the Native American woman on the English stage. Finally, neither Ferguson, Hendricks, nor Roach account for the destabilization and crisis of meaning through the blurring within and among political, historical, and cultural categories in Behn's colonial drama. In this chapter, I want to examine how *The Widow Ranter* conflates the problematic of divine right and the (falling) Stuart throne in England with the woman-as-land metaphor and the myth of Pocahontas in Virginia.

As Robert Markley argues, Behn promotes an idealized vision of royal authority and a benevolently paternalistic order which ironically liberates women from the demands of the patrilineal discourse on which it ultimately depends.[12] Throughout Behn's canon, as I also suggest in my work on Behn's *The Rover* parts 1 and 2, she fantasizes England's golden age as a period before the revolution of 1640, when royal authority was supposedly absolute.[13] This notion of England's golden age precedes the discourses of Puritanism and the new "individualism" which was, as Foucault argues in *The History of Sexuality*, an ideology of internalized sexual repression. In *The Widow Ranter*, the prelapsarian world of pre–civil war England—a world to which Behn longs to return—is grafted symbolically onto the Native American queen, her people, and her land. However, in contrast to Behn's optimistic and straightforward promotion of royalism in her earlier texts, in *The Widow Ranter*, as in *Oroonoko*, which were written after the Exclusion Crisis and probably immediately before James II's fall from power, Behn's vision of a quasi-utopian prelapsarian feminine world and a golden age of royal and divine authority is ambivalently rendered. Her beloved Stuart monarchy collapsed during this time, and as an avid Royalist, her world was in crisis.

A number of critics—such as Maureen Duffy, George Guffey, Janet Todd, and Laura Brown—have argued that *Oroonoko*, at least in part, is a political allegory about James II, Mary of Modena, and their heir, or about Charles I.[14] Recently, Joanna Lipking has countered these claims: "looking to . . . any political analogy provides no guide to the construction [of *Oroonoko*], which still appears arbitrary, patchy, formula-ridden."[15] I want to suggest that in *The*

*Widow Ranter* (and *Oroonoko*), Behn attempts to propagandize in favor of the Stuart crown, but because of the political turmoil of the times in which she writes, and because of her awareness of the potential ironies of supporting a patrilineal monarchy and male hereditary property rights, her discourse becomes beset by internal tensions. The result is a multiplicity of conflicting and overlapping positions about race, gender, and royal authority in these two works and, ultimately, a crisis in meaning. Like the male playwrights I have examined throughout this study, Behn attempts to resolve England's turbulent politics in her accounts of the New World—but because of the extraordinary political upheaval during the period in which she writes, and because of her own sense of despair in response to these events, she registers the chaos and confusion of her times.[16] The New World is portrayed as already fallen, already inaccessible, already contaminated and corrupted by Whigs and greedy white colonialists. As she herself recognizes, Behn both exposes and participates in the corrupt discourses of colonialism and expansionism.

This is not to say that a straightforward reading of historical events in the period provides a key to unlocking the complexities and ambiguities of *The Widow Ranter*. Instead, I want to suggest that reading history into or alongside *The Widow Ranter* makes clear the impossibility of finding fixed meaning in the play. Everything from English notions of "honor" to "race" are destabilized in *The Widow Ranter* in and by Behn's alteration of history. Indeed, this chapter will examine how Behn's transformation of "real" historical figures and events subverts stereotypical notions of gender, race, and culture. Most important to this study, these categories are subverted primarily through the figures of women—English and Native American. In *The Widow Ranter*, the feminized bodies of Virginia and England are complexly enmeshed in a tension-filled depiction of fallen royal power.

First it would be helpful to look at the play in the context of England's political turmoil at the end of the seventeenth century. For Behn, as well as many other writers between 1679 and 1689, the most significant political events were the Popish Plot and subsequent Exclusion Crisis and fall of the Stuart crown. Behn's response to Titus Oates plot, the Exclusion Bills, and the threat posed by Monmouth is depicted in the overt (and optimistic) Tory propaganda in her plays of the Exclusion period.[17] By the mid 1680s, however, political antipathy toward the Stuart crown grew far more intense. In 1687, the queen, Mary of Modena, announced she was pregnant. Until this time, it was believed that James was incapable of siring an heir, and the Protestant William of Orange (grandson of Charles I) would succeed to the throne. It was now feared that James's potential heir could ensure the future Catholic domination of England. Behn celebrated the king's heir in her "Congratulatory Poem to her

Most Sacred Majesty, on the Universal Hopes of All Loyal Persons for a Prince of Wales" (1688). By the end of the year, James had fled London, and William of Orange was invited by powerful Whig and Tory leaders to the throne of England.

Guffey argues that Behn's *Oroonoko* was written about the time that William's invitation was received in Holland; Todd suggests that it was most likely written between the announcement of the queen's pregnancy and her royal son's birth.[18] *The Widow Ranter* was probably written in 1687 or 1688, was first performed in 1689 (after Behn's death), and was published in 1690. In addition to Behn's acute sensitivity to the dangers of James's position during this time, her own health was failing. In effect, while writing *The Widow Ranter*, Behn's politics, beliefs, and her life itself, were all in crisis. The rifts and discontinuities in the sociopolitical discourse of *The Widow Ranter*, rather than artistic shortcomings, then, reflect Behn's profound concern with England's political crises during the 1680s.

The details of Nathaniel Bacon's rebellion and the history of the Virginia colony in the latter half of the seventeenth century also form an important backdrop to politics of gender, race, and class in *The Widow Ranter*. As Kathleen M. Brown argues, English politics, and the civil war in particular, had a prolonged and lasting effect on Virginia. The Virginia colony was a haven for Royalists in the seventeenth century; throughout the civil war period, Virginians remained loyal to the crown and it was the last colony to surrender to Cromwell. But the civil war also brought dissenters to Virginia, and, significantly, radicals were associated with women—outspoken, unruly women.[19] Governor Berkeley had been removed from his post during the civil war because of associations with the throne, but he was restored to power in 1660. Berkeley's return coincided with repression of religious dissenters, and this affected women Quakers, in particular, yet they remained steadfast in their outspokenness.[20] The difficulty for Berkeley's government in containing dissenting groups is reflected in its inability to repress female speech, and the threat of a small number of "women in each county who had crafted powerful communities through property ownership, legal learning, or reputations of defiance." Women who gossiped were the mouthpieces of their communities, and they became the voices of "moral authority" in the colony. Attempts to punish women who slandered were ineffective in suppressing female gossip.[21] Whipping and ducking, for example, proved unsuccessful in keeping women quiet.

Berkeley's government also had difficulty in keeping servants and slave laborers from provoking or participating in civil unrest. English servants in the colony were excluded from the body politic in order to ensure a large enough labor pool. Before 1675 more than half the population were either servants or slaves, "with English men making up the majority of unfree and newly freed individuals who, by the 1670s, were finding upward mobility more difficult." These men pressed their rights and protested their concerns with increasing force during this time. In 1667, Berkeley wrote to the king, " 'Consider us as a people press'd at our backes with Indians, in our Bowills with our servants . . . and invaded from without by Dutch.' "[22] The unrest of servant and slave reached dangerous levels during the 1660s and 1670s.[23] Several revolts by English servants were attempted at this time, which invoked memories of Cromwellian revolt in their masters. Other fears concerned servants who were former felons sent from England, and in 1670 all "convicts were banned from the colony." In 1671, attempts were made to keep Indian and African laborers under strict control. A 1672 act allowed the killing of African, Indian, and mulatto servants who ran away or committed crimes. Transported felons may also have caused unrest because they reported that conditions for English servants in England had improved. In Virginia, indentures lasted from four to seven years, whereas in England, many agricultural servants could renegotiate their contracts on a yearly basis, and they could find a new master if desired.[24] The longer periods of servitude encouraged abuses by masters in Virginia; instead of all-out rebellion, many servants simply ran away, exacerbating labor shortages. After mid-century, fears of servant unrest lead to the increased concern about connections between servants and slaves. Thus, distinctions between slave and servants were increasingly made from the mid to late seventeenth century onward.[25]

Virginia's governmental power in the second half of the seventeenth century was held in the hands of a small, elite group that did not shift as the colony expanded, making upward mobility almost impossible after 1660. This resulted in the alienation of both "wealthy newcomers and poorer freemen."[26] The colonial elite was made up of influential families whose arrival in Virginia dated to the 1640s and 1650s and who identified themselves as natives of the colony.[27] Antipathy toward this colonial elite, significantly, was directed at Berkeley's wife, Lady Frances Culpeper Stephens, whom he married in 1670. She was forty years old when he married her (thirty years his junior), and her relative youth provoked much mockery.[28] When the governor was popular, she was viewed positively, but when the government lost the support of smaller planters, many blamed Berkeley's wife. Her attention to cosmopolitan fashion was viewed as flaunting her wealth, and the governor's interest in Indian trade and his taking of a younger bride were seen as evidence of his greed.[29]

Individual counties, however, were ruled by lower-born country gentry. The lower-born members of the county government were despised by upper-class newcomers such as Nathaniel Bacon and his social clique. Bacon wrote:

Trace these men in Authority and Favour to whose hands the dispensation of the Countries wealth has been committed; let us observe the sudden Rise of their Estate compared with the Quality in which they first entered this Country Or the Reputation they have held here amongst wise and discerning men, And lett us see wither their extractions and Education have not bin vile.[30]

According to Bacon, only those born of noble descent in England should legitimately rule in Virginia. Bacon, a recent immigrant to Virginia, was the son of Thomas Bacon, a wealthy Suffolk squire. He attended Cambridge University for two years and studied law at Gray's Inn. He married Elizabeth Duke (who was disinherited as a result of the marriage), and because the couple were in need of income, his father sent him to Virginia with L1,800, in the hope that he would make his fortune in the New World. Bacon arrived alone in Virginia in 1674 at the age of twenty-four. He bought 1,230 acres of land on the frontier and established two plantations. As a gentleman, he was welcomed by Governor Berkeley, his cousin by marriage, and was honored with an appointment to the colony's council in 1675. Bacon sent for his wife soon after he settled. Berkeley, in contrast, had spent nearly thirty years of his life in Virginia and, at seventy, could have been Bacon's grandfather. Berkeley, like Bacon, had an elite educational background at the Inns of Court. But while Bacon's family "included a prominent parliamentarian advocate during the struggle against Charles I," Berkeley was a true-blue loyalist who had fought for the crown.[31]

Brown argues astutely that it was the combined alienation of the lower classes and the factionalism within the elite classes that fostered Bacon's rebellion. Twentieth-century historical accounts of Bacon's rebellion register the different perceptions of the political discord in the Virginia Colony. One widely held view is that Bacon was a political hero—a "torchbearer of democracy" who represented the people of Virginia in rebellion against the policies of the supposedly "tyrannical" royalist Governor Berkeley.[32] This view, however, depends on imposing a post-1776 democratic ideology on seventeenth-century controversies. In contrast, Wilcomb E. Washburn suggests that Bacon and his army did not fight against absolutism but against Indians and that his rebellion was not directly linked to the Whigs' political cause.[33]

The rebellion began in reaction to several Anglo-Indian conflicts on the frontier. Thomas Mathew's overseer was killed by a Doeg Indian in July 1675 in Stafford County. This attack led to the white colonists retaliating against both enemy Doeg and friendly Susquehannah Indians. Berkeley had spent thirty years forging friendly relations and alliances with some Indians and a policy of profitable and efficient exploitation of others. English newcomers, however, were unconcerned with the history of earlier relations with Indians. Frontier colonists were preoccupied with their own property and lives, and they found Berkeley's reluctance to battle all Indians outrageous. Later raids in 1675 by Susquehannahs resulted in the death of Bacon's overseer and one of William Byrd's servants. Even before the raids, Bacon and Bryd were at odds with Berkeley because he had prevented them from access to the profitable fur trade, which the governor monopolized. As a result of the Indian attacks, Berkeley's refusal to retaliate, and his monopoly of the fur trade, Bacon was persuaded to lead a group of angry backcountry men who wanted to take up arms against the Indians. Bacon's war against the Indians was viewed by Berkeley as a blatant usurpation of his authority, and this led to civil war within the colony.

Women—white and Indian—were crucial to the sociopolitics of Virginia during the rebellion. For the initial nine months of the rebellion, the momentum came from extralegal activities and networks, which depended largely on white women.[34] Bacon relied heavily on women's speech to help him recruit soldiers and support his activities. Women spread important information about Bacon's successes and attacked the governor's plans against Indians. These women included Mrs. Haviland, Mrs. Sarah Grendon, and Sarah Drummond. Loyalists to the governor also claimed women's voices among their followers. Lady Berkeley used similar techniques as the rebel women, and she was one of Bacon's staunchest enemies. She even went to England to explain her husband's activities to the king.

The rebels demonstrated their hostility toward the elite loyalists of the governor's supporters with violent treatment of women and children left behind to guard their large plantations. Colonel Hill, for example, who claimed to have suffered on this account wrote:

'To finish theire barbarisme, [the rebels] take my wife bigg w[i]th Child prisoner, beat her w[i]th my Cane, tare her Childbed linen out of her hands, and w[i]th her lead away my Children where they must live on corne and water and lye on the Ground.'[35]

Bacon's rebels thus subverted codes of proper treatment for upper-class women, especially pregnant upper-class women. Bacon also gathered and abducted "the prime mens wives, whos Husbands were with the Governour."[36] One observer wrote,

The poore Gent: Women were mightely astonish'd at this project; neather were there Husbands voide of amazements at this subtill invention. . . . This action was a Method, in war, that they were not well acquainted with (no not those the best inform'd in millitary affaires) that before they could com to pearce their enimies sides, they must be obliged to dart their wepons through there wives brest. . . . Whether it was these Considerations, or som others, I do not know, that kep their swords in their scabards.[37]

The abducted white women represented the badges of upper-class loyalist men: they were referred to as "white aprons," which distinguished them from white and black women who labored in the tobacco fields in rougher fabric.[38] Bacon's abduction and possession of the "white aprons" represented his power over the male Virginia aristocrats.

Bacon succeeded in burning and taking possession of Jamestown, but he died suddenly in October 1676, and the rebellion ended with him. By the end of 1676, Berkeley controlled the colony once again.[39] Berkeley regained control by attacking rebel estates and hanging their leaders. Women were not spared from the governor's violence. Four rebel women were imprisoned, another woman died after delivering a stillborn child when the governor's servants attacked her home, and the sexual reputations of rebel women were attacked by the governor as well.[40] Wives of rebel prisoners were often prevented from bringing food to their husbands. Berkeley also confiscated estates of a number of rebels, leaving their wives and children homeless.[41] But the arrival of the king's commissioners put an end to the governor's revenge and reestablished the crown as the most important source of political power in the colony.

The king's commissioners were eager, in particular, to restore positive relations with friendly Pamunkey Indians who were led by an Indian queen—Cockacoeske. Cockacoeske and her tribe had been brutalized and violated by Bacon in August 1676 in order to acquire her tribe's land. The narratives of Bacon's final battles reaffirm the mythology of Pocahontas: the taming of the native woman again functions as a model of successful English colonialism. Cockacoeske ruled Powhatan's chiefdom from 1656 until her death in the 1680s. She worked within the framework of the legal system of the colonial government, and in March 1676, she agreed to provide Pamunkey guides and spies to aid the colonial government in their defense against hostile tribes. Her initial "tearful" reluctance to assist the colonial government stemmed from the loss of her late husband and one hundred Pamunkey men who died while helping the colonial government in an earlier defense against hostile Indians.[42] Cockacoeske had a biracial child, John West, the son of Colonel West; her son may have acted as a go-between and helped to established positive relations between the Pamunkeys and the colonial government.[43]

Because of the peace agreement Cockacoeske established with the colonial government in March 1676, she told her people to flee rather than retaliate when Bacon later attacked her tribe. In this first attack, the only Indian deaths that occurred were that of a small child and an old woman (later another old woman who would not lead Bacon and his men to Cockacoeske was also killed). Soon after, Bacon found the Cockacoeske's hiding place and killed forty five of her people. She escaped, but her belongings, which she valued greatly, were stolen. After Bacon's attack, Cockacoeske intended to surrender, but upon finding a dead Indian woman killed by Bacon's army, she was greatly frightened and wandered alone in the wilderness for fourteen days. She afterward petitioned the colonial government for the return of her goods, although they disregarded her request.[44]

After Bacon's death, the king's commission found that Cockacoeske had been wronged by Bacon and by the colonial government, and she was given many valuable objects as compensation for her losses.[45] Further, she proved to be a powerful agent in establishing a new peace treaty between the colony and several tidewater Indian tribes. The figure of Cockacoeske, then, resembles previous conflicted images of Native American women which I have examined in this study: she is both benevolent and dangerous, necessary to the colonial government and feared/hated by the rebels.

The consequences of Bacon's rebellion to Virginia society were enormous. Servants and slaves were no longer viewed as docile and controllable after 1677, the lower classes had tasted power which they would not forget, and white women were viewed as powerful political agents who needed to be controlled. These women's acts of spreading news, guarding estates, or bringing food to imprisoned rebels were crucial to the colony.[46] Not surprisingly, women were blamed for the rebellion as well. Many rebels claimed it was the pleas of their wives and children that drove them to take part in the war.[47]

Ironically, then, in the postrebellion period, women were turned into passive victims of war, and Bacon's worst crimes were heralded as those against women. Philip Ludwell wrote that Bacon's rebels went about "Ravishing woemen and Children from their houses and hurrying them about the Country in their Rude Camp and often threatening them with death, because their husbands and fathers obeyed his Ma[jes]ties Lawfull Power."[48] In the royal commissioner's reports to the king, all colonial women were turned into submissive victims—even rebel women, powerful female loyalists such as Lady Berkeley, and the Pamunkey queen.[49]

Racial distinctions were more firmly delineated in Virginia as a result of the rebellion, racism against nonwhites increased, and interracial sex was viewed as more taboo. Claims of interracial sexual activity, for example, were used as a means of attacking former Bacon rebels.[50] In the rebellion, slaves and indentured servants had joined together to fight for Bacon, and, significantly, the last group to surrender was made up of black slaves and white servants. Planters thus needed to ensure that white servants did not ally themselves with blacks and Indians. All Indians taken captive after 1677 were made slaves. Over the next few years, Indians and blacks were thrown together into one legal category, which restricted them to perpetual slavery if their parents were not of Christian countries at the period of their initial purchase.[51] They were increasingly denied any status or privileges as free people. As I described in the Introduction, white women who attempted to intermarry, or who bore mixed-race children, suffered severe punishments after 1691.

The roles of women and people of color in Virginia immediately before, during, and after the Bacon rebellion are crucial to understanding Behn's *Widow Ranter*. In the play, Behn draws on and distorts images of the Indian queen Cockoescke, Lady Berkeley and other women loyalists, the outspoken women religious dissenters, and the female rebel advocates in the Bacon conflict. Behn's process of surrogation nostalgically marks the impossibility of replicating the Pocahontas/Rolfe union, yet the restaging of these different colonial women also highlights the crucial roles of women—white, Indian, and black—in the colony. Behn's play also attempts to transcend white class conflicts at work in Virginia by displacing them into a comedic theatrical setting. Behn interconnects the above historical events and figures in Virginia with contemporary sociopolitics in England, including the Exclusion Crisis, and the fall of James II.

*The Widow Ranter* distorts and alters the historical accounts of the 1676 rebellion in disturbing and complex ways.[52] To begin with, Behn makes Bacon a (wifeless) romantic hero who fights for love, not for land, property, or power (at least not overtly). Bacon loves Behn's version of the Indian queen, who is married and claims she cannot honorably allow herself to consummate her desire for Bacon. Interestingly, Behn conflates the Pocahontas tale with the story of Cockacoeske. Behn's Semernia says she loved Bacon from the first time they met, when she was twelve years old. It was about this same age that Pocahontas met and befriended Captain John Smith. When Pocahontas finally married John Rolfe, she was, like Semernia, previously married to the Indian man Kocoum. Semernia's marriage to Cavernio is problematic in terms of her feelings for Bacon, but in Pocahontas's case, her previous marital condition apparently had no effect on the union with Rolfe. However, despite the similarities between Behn's Indian queen and Pocahontas, Semernia's relationship with the Virginians is much more like Cockacoeske's (and her tribe's) relationship with the colonists than Pochahontas's. Semernia and Cavernio are on friendly terms with the white Virginians. The earlier Powhatans were not. Also, Semernia's hiding in the forest to escape Bacon seems to draw on Cockacoeske's attempt to flee Bacon. Yet, the Pamunkey queen was not killed by Bacon—indeed, although he killed many of her people and stole her goods, she did not surrender to him, and after his death she went on to wield significant power as an intermediary between many tidewater tribes and the colonial government.[53] Semernia, in contrast, runs from her passion for the white man and dies.

Behn's portrait of Semernia thus draws on the postrebellion Virginian views of colonial women—especially white women—as passive victims of the war, as well as the conventions of love and honor plays. Despite the Pamunkey queen's and many of the white women of Virginia's powerful leadership capabilities, as I have shown, they repeatedly are depicted as weak and needing white male protection. Semernia is described as a "tim'rous Dove" (I.i.109) without "Amazonian fire" (V.i.192) who is doomed from the start.[54] Semernia remarks how,

> [t]he more I gaze upon this English Stranger [Bacon], the more Confusion struggles in my Soul: Oft I have heard of Love, and oft this Gallant Man (when peace had made him pay his idle Visits) Has told a thousand Tales of dying Maids. And ever when he spoke, my panting Heart, with a Prophetick fear in sighs reply'd, I shall fall such a Victim to his Eyes.
>
> (II.i.38–42)

Semernia's "confusion" about her love for Bacon suggests that she is torn between her political and familial allegiances. Should she remain true to her husband/king, or should she follow her passion for Bacon? Bacon's love, as Sermenia "prophecies," requires her to become his "victim" and deny her own culture, identity, and self. When she asks Bacon, "what is the God of Love?" (II.i.130), he explains,

> 'Tis a resistless Fire, that's kinddled thus— . . . at every gaze we take from fine Eyes, from such Bashfull Looks, and such soft touches—it makes us sigh—and pant as I do now, and stops Breath when e're we speak of Pain. . . . It makes us tremble, when we touch the fair one. . . . The Eyes are dying, and the Cheeks are pale, The tongue is faltring, and the body fainting.
>
> (II.i.131–134, 136, 138–139)

Bacon's passion for Semernia is linked to physical pain and torture. The white man's desire for the native woman and her land is devastating and uncontrollable: he must possess his lover no matter what the cost. Behn recognizes that the Indians in Virginia were doomed and Sermernia's predicament functions as a symbol of their fate.

Semernia has no choice but to suffer and die: to deny her passion for Bacon is a kind of death, but to act on her feelings for Bacon is dishonorable. The Indian queen's command reflects her internal weakness and emotional and physical entrapment: "take all our Kingdoms—make our People Slaves, and let me fall beneath your Conquering Sword: but never let me hear you talk again, or gaze upon my Eyes" (II.i.142–149). For Semernia, death is the only solution to their taboo love, and she therefore wills her own demise. She has no alternative but to give everything, including her life, to Bacon; like Pocahontas, if she does not give herself, she knows that she will be taken anyway.

After the death of the Indian king, Semernia hides deep in the wilderness to avoid becoming Bacon's "Fair Captive" (IV.ii.60), and disguises herself from Bacon by wearing the costume of a male warrior. At the end of the battle, Semernia's servant Anaria announces, "the Wood's surrounded by the Conqueror. . . . [W]hat he cannot gain by soft submission, Force will at last o'ercome" (V.i.166–167, 173–174). These words echo the colonists' treatment of the Indians in early colonial Virginia. But, in striking contrast to Cockoeske, who also ran and hid from Bacon, Sermernia falls victim, or makes herself victim, to the white rebel's sword. As Bacon comes nearer, one of Semernia's soldiers tells her that Bacon "demands the Queen with such a voice, and Eyes so Fierce and Angry, he kills us with his Looks" (V.i.198–199). When Bacon attacks Semernia and her soldiers, she cries "Hold! Hold, I do Command ye . . . —hold thy commanding Hand, and do not kill me, who wou'd not hurt thee to regain my Kingdom" (V.i.204–206). In this instance, Semernia's passive resistance leads to her death and the destruction of her people. She is pleased to fall by Bacon's hand: as she dies, she tells Bacon that his killing her is "The noblest office of a Gallant Friend, thou'st sav'd my Honour, and has given me Death" (V.i.211–212). Semernia sees Bacon's violent attack as redemptive. Like the Indian Boy and Girl in Dryden's Prologue to the *Indian Queen* who long to be conquered by the white colonist, Behn's native woman ultimately views her death and the relinquishing of her property and people as morally necessary. As we have seen earlier, there are competing notions of honor in the colony.

The responsibility for the violence of colonialism, therefore, is displaced onto the familiar form of the Indian woman who invites her own death. While Semernia acts sexually "honorably" in one sense—she will not break her vow to her husband and king for her love of another (white) man; yet, in doing so, she destroys herself and her people altogether. After all, if she were to marry Bacon after Cavernio's death (in a Pocahontas/Rolfe-like gesture), she might save her tribe. Thus her concern with honor leads not only to her own death, but to the defeat of her people as well. Behn's version of Bacon's rebellion thus recasts the old tale of blame for the evils of colonialism onto Semernia, but it also suggests that female honor in itself is problematic and dangerous not only for women, but for the English and colonial cultures at large.[55]

Semernia's death also registers contemporary views of interracial sex and
the Anglo-Indian cultural assimilation in Virginia. As I discussed in the Introduction, after Pocahontas's death and certainly by the late seventeenth century, the Pocahontas/Rolfe union was no longer a viable method of colonization. Instead, as historians repeatedly point out, by this time all-out violence
was held as necessary to the maintenance of English prosperity in Virginia:
the availability of white wives had increased and miscegenation was illegal.
Moreover, the rebellion itself reflected intense colonial racism that only increased at the war's end. In Behn's vision, the fated love between Bacon and
Semernia thus reproduces contemporary colonial discourse and law which assert that the Pochahontas/Rolfe union is a nostalgic and tragic fantasy that can
no longer be fulfilled and which denies the existence of powerful Indian
women of the North American coastal tribes who resist colonial domination.
Behn's doomed interracial union might be seen, then, as recasting and repro-
ducing fears about the loss of Englishness through interracial contact, and the
fear of overpowering Indian women—Bacon appears to go native precisely
because he becomes an unruly subject in his pursuit of Semernia.

I want to suggest that the tragic portrayal of the love between Bacon and
Semernia in *The Widow Ranter* is also enmeshed in Behn's obsessive preoc-
cupation with the fall of the Stuart crown. From this angle, Bacon might
function as an antihero, a Cromwellian or parliamentarian rebel in dangerous
pursuit of the throne, and the death of Sermernia and Cavernio would reflect
the evils of usurpation. As one of the government's council fears, in winning
Semernia, Bacon would become king in Virginia.

> Whim[sey]. . . . I am afraid that under pretence of killing all the Indians [Ba-
> con] means to Murder us, ly with our Wives, and hang up our little Children,
> and make himself Lord and King.
> Whiff. Brother *Whimsey* . . . *Bacon* came seasonably to our Aid, and what he
> has done was for our defence, the *Indians* came down upon us, and Ravisht
> us all, Men, Women, and Children. . . .
> Down[right]. 'Tis most certain that *Bacon* did not demand a Commission out
> of a design of serving us, but to satisfy his Ambition and his Love; it being
> no secret that he passionately Admires the Indian *Queen*, and under the pre-
> text of War, intends to kill the King her Husband, Establish himself in her
> Heart, and on all occasions make himself a more formidable Enemy than the
> *Indians* are.
>
> (I.ii.6–13, 19–24)

Despite the unreliability of Downright and Whimsey, Bacon's pursuit of the
Indian queen, and the possibility that he might win her and take Cavernio's
place, accentuates the dangers of Bacon's rebellion in *The Widow Ranter*. In-

deed, after killing Sermernia, Bacon kills himself as he comes to realize that his pursuit of the queen conflates political usurpation with love. Dying, Bacon says to Daring, "now while you are Victors, make a Peace—with the English Councel—and never let Ambition—Love—or Interest make you forget as I have done—your Duty—and Allegiance—farewel—a long farewel—" (V.i.306–309). Bacon suggests that duty to the colonial government, and hence allegiance to the Stuart throne, is necessary for the colony's survival.

Yet Bacon's speech about the necessity to honor one's government is undermined throughout the play by the conspicuous alteration of historical events in the absence of the royalist Governor Berkeley. Surely contemporary audiences would react strongly to the missing Berkeley, with his steadfastly loyal connections to the Stuarts. In this regard, Behn constructs a Virginia that resembles England's civil war era, or perhaps more pointedly, a contemporary England which soon will, or has already, dethroned its rightful heir, James II. Behn's profound concern for the problem of the absence of a legitimate ruler, and her puzzling attempt to resolve or at least mark it, is evidenced in that she uses this device in both *Oroonoko* and *The Widow Ranter*. In Behn's version of Bacon's story, comically inept justices of the peace abuse their power as the people of the colony wait for the "Nobly Born" and "Gallant" lord governor to arrive and "make [Virginia] one of the best Colonies in the World" (I.i.103–104). The colony of Virginia in *The Widow Ranter*, like that of Surinam in *Oroonoko*, "for want of a Governour . . . [is] Ruled by a Councill, some of which have been perhaps transported Criminals, who having Acquired great Estates, are now become your Honour and Right Worshipful and possess all Places of Authority" (I.i.106–110). Thus Bacon is set up, on the one hand as a dangerous usurper, and on the other hand as a much needed alternative ruler for the colony, a stand-in for the absent stand-in of the Stuart monarch. As Friendly says, Bacon describes himself as a "Romulus" or "Alexander," (I.i.118), to which Hazard replies, "great souls are born in commen men sometimes as well as Princes" (I.i. 120–121). Similarly, Oroonoko is an odd combination of a black slave (renamed, significantly, "Caesar") and a prince. Thus, for Behn, the governor's (or legitimate ruler's) absence in *The Widow Ranter* (and *Oroonoko*), and the ensuing sociopolitical chaos in the colony (honorable men usurp authority, but the authority usurped is hardly honorable because the "true" king is absent and the lower-born rule), serve as crucial markers of the destabilization of political legitimacy in England of the 1680s. Behn registers this sociopolitical confusion in her ambiguous and highly vexed portrayal of Bacon himself.

In another twist of historical and dramatic conflations, the tragic failure of the Sermernia/Bacon interracial union could serve as yet one more indication of the problem of the absence of the Governor Berkeley in the play. According to historical accounts, Berkeley had worked for years to establish friendly and economically productive relations with the Native Americans before Bacon arrived in Virginia. As I explained earlier in this chapter, Berkeley was well-known for his Indian-friendly policies and his links to Cockacoeske, the Pamunkey queen. In historical accounts, Bacon's rebellion against Berkeley led to all-out attacks on the Indians, including, quite significantly, the Pamunkeys. Thus the impossibility of interracial love in Behn's play might be seen as another tragic marker of the enormous cost of the governor's/legitimate ruler's absence. In both historical records and *The Widow Ranter*, colonial political usurpation hurts a royal Indian woman and her people. In effect, in *The Widow Ranter*, Indians are murdered and heroes "lose their heads" and die because the loyalist governor and the crown he represents are absent. Notions of gender, race, and class are destabilized by Behn's historical alterations and inversions, because the deaths of Semernia and Cavernio represent both the losses suffered in the Americas as a result of the fall of the crown and the death of the Stuart crown itself.

The blurring of racial, gender, and class categories in Behn's alteration of history extends to white women in the play as well. In historical accounts, women's power and the abuse of women by men constitutes a large part of the rebellion. Thus, usurpation of political authority (even with the governor present) takes place by and through colonial female bodies. But the rebellion also depends in large measure, as I have demonstrated, on the power of female speech and unruly women. Behn picks up on the postrebellion theme of female victimization and the attempted repression of female power, as we have seen with Semernia and with the abduction of loyalist wives in the play, but she also juxtaposes the role(s) of the female victim to the fictional character of the Widow Ranter, a figure who is composed of an amalgamation of potent women of different races and classes. Ranter's name harks back to the unruly, outspoken dissenting women from the civil war era in England, and to the women whose speech and power cannot be controlled by Berkeley's government in the colony. In addition, she resembles the outspoken and verbally instrumental Lady Berkeley, who also married a much older man. Like Lady Berkeley, she engages successfully in political activities through her negotiations with Daring and Madame Surelove and battles adroitly in the rebellion itself.

In an odd twist for the class-conscious Behn, however, Ranter is a positively portrayed lower-born woman, a former servant who moved up the social scale by marrying her now-deceased former master. Her behavior reveals her social background—she drinks, swears, and smokes a pipe, but she also negotiates her desires effectively and remains, in contrast to all of the other female characters in the play, uncontrolled and unvictimized by men. Ranter thus is portrayed, I would argue, in favorable terms. She is the title character after all, named before Bacon or his rebellion. The elevation of the lower-class Ranter thus functions as one more sign of the destabilization of social categories in Behn's play. As discussed earlier in this chapter, Bacon's rebellion occurs *because* the lower-classes rule, yet in Ranter's case, the upward mobility of the lower-class is depicted favorably.

Ranter's cross-dressing as a man further highlights the destabilization of meaning in the play. In cross-dressing, Ranter registers contemporary anxieties about the problem of racial amalgamation and miscegenation and anxieties about the destabilization of class structure. As Marjorie Garber writes, gender cross-dressing can function as *"a space of possibility structuring and confounding culture*: [it is] the disruptive element that intervenes, not just as a category crisis of male and female, but the crisis of category itself."[56] I believe Ranter's act of cross-dressing is Behn's attempt to consolidate the disparate and confused sociopolitical, gender, and racial discourses of her age. Interestingly, in many of Behn's works, cross-dressing for women, and the issue of women donning a male identity, functions as a means of asserting female authority and critiquing rigid gender roles.[57] With Ranter, Behn brings together servant women (who are crucially suggestive of the large numbers of black female slaves imported to Virginia at this time who were rapidly replacing white female indentured servants so that white women could become "white aprons"), religious dissenters, and upper-class women. In effect, through the linking of disparate socioeconomic, political, racial, and gendered identities in Ranter's body, Behn attempts to resolve, or at least unify, the intense social and political oppositions at war in the late seventeenth century in England and Virginia. It is not surprising, however, that Ranter can only be figured as a joke, or a mockery. It seems significant that while Ranter humorously wields a phallic sword, Semernia and Cavernio are killed by one. And, while Ranter rises socially and economically, African and Indian women (although they are conspicuously offstage) are the victims of her elevation. Finally, and above all, Ranter's hybridity, her blurring of distinctions, calls attention to the crisis of categories—for she is a blatant dramatic invention in an historically "real" context.

The problematic of cross-dressing in *The Widow Ranter* also reflects anxieties about staging the other woman in the seventeenth century. Cross-dressing, performing the other gender, is attempted by both Indian (Semernia) and white women (Ranter) in the play. Behn demonstrates that being looked-at, being staged, has its high price for the Indian woman. Semernia and her female servant Anaria repeatedly say Bacon's "looks" kill them. Semernia tries to escape this problem by cross-dressing as an Indian man, but she fails and dies. This failure has several possible veiled meanings: one can never escape being Indian, hence one can never survive in white theatrical and/or colonial contexts whether male or female; (for white women) playing the Indian onstage has the same dangerous consequences as "going native" in the real world; (for white women) playing the native onstage is impossible and unbelievable, and can only result in a flawed performance. Most playwrights of the seventeenth century, perhaps for the above reasons, do not bring their Indian women onstage. As we have seen throughout this study, except in the case of Dryden, where interracial love does not involve English men, the native woman remains in shadow—desired, dangerous, rarely seen, never touched. Behn brings Semernia (Pocahontas/Cockacoeske) onstage, but she kills her. Even with all the symbolic links to the Stuart crown, Semernia's death is unsettling, and her phantasmatic white double, Ranter, functions as a chilling stand-in, an eerie mimic of the Indian and black women on whose backs she rises.

Looking back to Bacon's rebellion itself, the vexed sign of the sword Behn's Ranter tries to wield makes (no) sense: more than anything, the rebellion was a battle for money and power between white men. Berkeley himself had offered to duel with Bacon. Behn takes this metaphor and turns it upside down in three inter-racial and/or inter-gender duels: between Cavernio and Bacon, between Semernia and Bacon, and between Ranter and Daring. The first two end in the deaths of the Indians, the third leads to love and the attempted unification of disparate social forces. This swordplay reflects yet more undoing of meaning in the text. The sword ultimately signifies lack or absence of meaning for Behn, as does the falling aristocratic social class that it represents. Ranter, the woman dressed as a man, uses her lack to some advantage. Bacon, in contrast, who does not lack, dies. Behn seems to want to supplement notions of male supremacy and authority with the concept that the white female performance of phallic power can supersede fact, history, or "truth." For Behn, then, above all else, the theater of history, gender, and race in *The Widow Ranter* marks the destabilization of fixed meaning, the blurring of categories and boundaries, and, hence, the impossibility of performing the always and already fictional "real."

# Afterword

As this study has shown, the ambivalence of colonial contact becomes heightened at the end of the seventeenth century, and anxieties about the New World are transferred increasingly from the native woman onto the English woman. From the Restoration and well into the eighteenth century, the "proper" domestic English woman is constructed *against* images of the other woman as savage, sexually dangerous, and uncontained, and fears about the invasion of otherness and the loss of an idealized pure English identity are linked with a tainted and degraded white female body. In eighteenth-century literature and culture, as Felicity Nussbaum and Laura Brown demonstrate, the white woman's deviant body—from the coquette to the prostitute—takes the blame for the evils of colonialism by embodying the negative aspects of imperialism. At the close of the seventeenth century, then, the native and other woman are no longer viewed as marriageable for English men, and the fantasy of interracial romance of the Pocahontas myth becomes, at best, a lost ideal.[1] Southerne's dramatic adaptation of *Oroonoko* (1696), Richard Steele's prose redaction of the Inkle and Yarico tale in *The Spectator* 11 (13 March 1711), and Henry Neville's *Isle of Pines* (1668), reflect the ambivalence of the redactions of the Pocahontas and Malinche myths, the woman-as-land metaphor, and the discursive attempt to eliminate interracial romance.

Southerne's dramatic adaptation of Aphra Behn's *Oroonoko* most strikingly demonstrates the fall of the fantasy of interracial romance as well as the projection of savagery onto the European woman. Southerne constructs an interracial romance where there was none: in his version Imoinda is white. Other than her change in skin color, however, very little about her is different—

she remains passive and loyal. In effect, Imoinda is black in white face—thus blurring and confusing distinctions between the European and African woman. In her maternal function, Imoinda represents the threat of interracial romance: she cannot produce a white European child. Oroonoko says her womb is dark and that he cannot bring his child to "light." In this sense, Imoinda is a scapegoat for the child's hybridity. Thus, her difference from Oroonoko (and from herself) dooms the lovers and marks both her desirability and danger to all, black and white. In Southerne's version, Imoinda is loved by the white lieutenant governor, and he intends to have her at any cost, even though she is married and pregnant with Oroonoko's child. As in Behn's tale, the two lovers prefer death over slavery, and particularly over the loss of possession of Imoinda's body and their heir through slavery. Imoinda kills herself—she presses the dagger to her own heart because Oroonoko cannot. She appropriately self-destructs because of the crime of interracial romance. In this instance a black prince cannot be allowed to marry a white/black woman, and thus their hybrid child (black/white, royal/nonroyal) has no place in late seventeenth-century English culture and cannot occupy a conceptual space of representation.

Neville's novella, *The Isle of Pines*, draws heavily on the tradition of woman as representative of the land of the New World, and looks forward to Defoe's domestication and feminization of nature in *Robinson Crusoe*. As in many of the works I have examined, there are no natives left on the narrator's island. The narrator impregnates three women with whom he has been shipwrecked— a mother, her daughter, and their black slave—and "peoples" the island in the New World, primarily with whites but also with the children of the black woman. In this instance, interracial sexual contact looks forward to a future economy based on slavery. The children from the narrator's different sexual liaisons are kept separate—possibly for the avoidance of incest, but also to maintain racial and class distinctions. Implicit in the narrator's reluctant sexual relationship with the black woman is the need and desire for the production of worker-slaves in his new colony.

Finally, Steele's tale of Inkle and Yarico replicates and then fully revises the tale of Pocahontas. Inkle, like John Smith, is saved by the native woman in the New World. They become lovers and she becomes pregnant. Inkle promises to take her with him when he leaves their love nest, but when they rejoin the Europeans he sells Yarico into slavery. Here, as in Neville's tale, interracial sexual contact is useful only so long as it is economically effective. The Inkle and Yarico tale performs a solution to the problem of white male desire for the other woman by translating interracial romance into economic productivity.

At the close of the seventeenth century, then, desire for and fear of the native woman and woman of color appears to be transformed into a (seemingly distinctive) material and productive interest. If we see the other woman, and if we see her engaged sexually with a white man, it is for the exclusive purpose of (re)production of slave labor. Hybridity is subsumed into slavery—the whiteness of the interracial children ceases to exist under the yoke of their darker heredity.

The longing for and fear of Pocahontas and interracial romance is never fully exhumed from our white American cultural texts, however, even in the twentieth century. We continue to be captivated by the ambivalence of interracial love in contemporary American film and TV. Oprah's talking positively about it, TV shows and TV movies (more than feature films) abound with it, and so on. Yet when interracial relationships are shown, they are depicted in ways that minimize the history of racial and class differences. Disney's *Pocahontas* (1995), in particular, marks a conservative replaying of this tale. Although the film demonstrates a proto-ecological portrait of the English destruction of the New World, and offers a proto-feminist Pocahontas who must choose her own man, it concludes with a traditional anti-interracial ending. Pocahontas stays home, the wounded John Smith goes back to England to be healed by western doctors, and there is no husband, John Rolfe, to mark Pocahontas's incorporation into a white colonialist world.

The ambivalence of Pocahontas goes on, however. Her tale never fully disappears. The Pocahontas of *Disney's Pocahontas II: Journey to a New World* (1998) goes to England, as a representative of her people, to meet the English king. But, on her arrival, she finds that the king is about to send an Armada to attack the Powhatans. Pocahontas succeeds in stopping the Armada, and in the process, John Rolfe and Pocahontas fall in love. Rolfe ultimately gives up his civilized life in England (and a plum position with the crown) and returns with her by ship to live in Virginia. This version of the Pocahontas story inverts the tale of her abduction and colonization by suggesting it is Rolfe who willingly and happily goes native: he cannot resist *her*. While *Pocahontas II* offers, in some measure, a more optimistic view of interracial relations than its Disney predecessor, it simultaneously obscures the brutal history of the destruction of Native Americans in Virginia. The myth of Pocahontas and the woman-as-land metaphor continues to evolve, then—it has no end and it tells no truth other than to register our ongoing anxieties about the blurring of gender, race, culture, and ethnicity.

# Notes

## Introduction

1. On the relationship of women, science, and nature, see Carolyn Merchant, *The Death of Nature: Women, Ecology, and the Scientific Revolution* (New York: Harper and Row, 1989). On the woman-as-land metaphor see, for example, Annette Kolodny, *The Lay of the Land: Metaphor as Experience and History in American Life and Letters* (Chapel Hill: University of North Carolina Press, 1975); Gary Nash Smith, *Virgin Land: The American West as Symbol and Myth* (Cambridge, Mass.: Harvard University Press, 1950); Anne Mclintock, *Imperial Leather: Race, Gender, and Sexuality in the Colonial Contest* (New York: Routledge, 1995); Mary Louise Pratt, *Imperial Eyes: Travel Writing and Transculturation*, (London: Routledge Press, 1992); Peter Hulme, *Colonial Encounters: Europe and the Native Caribbean 1492–1797* (1986; reprint, London: Routledge, 1992).

2. Pratt, *Imperial Eyes*, 57.

3. I have borrowed Joan Wallach Scott's notion of gender as an "organizing" function in a social structure, but I have added race as a crucial part of this "organizing" function; see Scott's, *Gender and the Politics of History* (New York: Columbia University Press, 1988), 27.

4. Natalie Zemon Davis, "Women On Top," in *Society and Culture in Early Modern France* (Stanford: Stanford University Press, 1975), 124, 127.

5. Earl Miner argues, for example, that the theatrical symbol of the wild man of the New World functioned as a mirror to the English of the wildness within themselves (97), in "The Wild Man through the Looking Glass," in *The Wild Man Within: An Image in Western Thought from Renaissance to Romanticism*, ed. Dudley Moore and Maximillian Novak (Pittsburgh: University of Pittsburgh Press, 1972).

6. See Edward W. Said, *Orientalism* (New York: Vintage, 1979), 65. Although *Orientalism* has been extensively critiqued, Said's notion of "staging" the other for European audiences is useful to my argument in this instance.

7. Hayden White, "The Forms of Wildness: Archaeology of an Idea," in *Tropics of Discourse: Essays in Cultural Criticism* (Baltimore: John Hopkins University Press, 1978), 151, 152.

8. In regard to Restoration redactions and adaptations of *The Tempest*, which I discuss in chapter 2, Miner argues that the theatrical representations of the New World provided the "people of the audience . . . [with] a topsy turvy world which is righted at last . . . when male dominance and class distinctions are reinstated" ("Wild Man," 101). Miner also argues that seventeenth-century theories of government are defined through Restoration theatrical representations of the wild man in the New World ("Wild Man," 97, 99).

9. Ania Loomba, *Gender, Race, Renaissance Drama* (Manchester: Manchester University Press, 1992); Kim F. Hall, *Things of Darkness: Economies of Race and Gender in Early Modern England* (Ithaca: Cornell University Press, 1995); Margo Hendricks and Patricia Parker, "Introduction," in *Women, "Race," and Writing in the Early Modern Period*, ed. Margo Hendricks and Patricia Parker (London: Routledge, 1994); the complete volume of essays in *Women, "Race," & Writing in the Early Modern Period*; Margaret Ferguson, "News From the New World: Miscegenous Romance in Aphra Behn's *Oroonoko* and *The Widow Ranter*," *The Production of English Renaissance Culture*, ed. David Lee Miller (Ithaca: Cornell University Press, 1994); Laura Brown, *Ends of Empire: Women and Ideology in Early Eighteenth-Century English Literature* (Ithaca: Cornell University Press, 1993); Felicity Nussbaum, *Torrid Zones: Maternity, Sexuality, and Empire in Eighteenth-Century English Narratives* (Baltimore: Johns Hopkins University Press, 1995); Charlotte Sussman, *Consuming Anxieties: Consumer Protest, Gender, and British Slavery* (Stanford: Stanford University Press, 2000); Moira Ferguson, *Subject to Others: British Women Writers and Colonial Slavery, 1670–1834* (New York: Routledge Press, 1992); Bridget Orr, *Empire on the English Stage, 1660–1714* (Cambridge: Cambridge University Press, forthcoming); Srinivas Aravamudan, *Tropicopolitans: Colonialism and Agency, 1699–1804 (Post-Contemporary Interventions)* (Durham, N.C.: Duke University Press, 1999); and Joseph Roach, *Cities of the Dead: Circum-Atlantic Performance* (New York: Columbia University Press, 1996). Roach's stunning work on gender, race, and performance in *Cities of the Dead* greatly helped my thinking about performing the other in the seventeenth century.

For other important critical work on the overlapping discourses of race and gender in Restoration and eighteenth-century literature see, for example, Peter Hulme, *Colonial Encounters*; Carol Barash, "The Character of Difference: The Creole Woman as Cultural Mediator in Narratives about Jamaica," in *Eighteenth-Century Studies* 23 (1990): 406–424; Rosalind Ballaster, "New Histericism: Aphra Behn's Oroonoko: The Body, the Text, and the Feminist Critic," in *New Feminist Discourses*, ed. Isobel Armstrong (New York: Routledge Press, 1993), 283–295; Felicity Nussbaum, "The Politics of Difference: Introduction," *Eighteenth-Century Studies* 23 (1990): 375–386; Charlotte Sussman, "The Other Problem with Women: Reproduction and Slave Culture in Aphra Behn's *Oroonoko*," in *Rereading Aphra Behn: History, Theory, and Criticism*, ed. Heidi Hutner (Charlottesville: University Press of Virginia, 1993), 212–233; Nancy Armstrong and Leonard Tennenhouse, *The Imaginary Puritan: Literature, Intellectual Labor, and the Origins of Personal Life*

(Berkeley: University of California Press, 1992); and Firdous Azim, *The Colonial Rise of the Novel* (London: Routledge, 1993).

10. Orr extends this point to include all genres of Restoration literature. She states that "very little attention has been directed to the nationalist and colonialist dimensions of literary culture in the Restoration" (Orr, *Empire*, forthcoming). Orr's impressive study of colonialism in Restoration drama differs greatly from mine— she takes a far more broad approach—examining questions of empire well beyond the North American territories, and she does not focus on the figure of the colonial or native woman.

11. Nicholas Jose, *Ideas of the Restoration in English Literature, 1660–71* (Cambridge, Mass.: Harvard University Press, 1984), 1. See also J. P. Kenyon, who argues that in the early Restoration there was a strong desire to turn the clock back to 1641, to the "status quo ante bellum." In *Stuart England* (England: Penguin, 1988), 196, 209–210.

12. Brown, *Ends of Empire*, 4.

13. Merchant, *Death of Nature*, 131.

14. Ibid., 131–132.

15. Ibid., 146.

16. Christopher Columbus, *The Four Voyages of Christopher Columbus*, ed. and trans. J. M. Cohen (London: Penguin, 1969), 218; S. E. Morison, *Admiral of the Ocean Sea: A Life of Christopher Columbus* (Boston, 1942), 308, quoted in Hulme, *Colonial Encounters*, 159; George Chapman, "De Guiana carmen Epicum," in Richard Hakluyt, *The Principal Navigations, Voyages, Traffiques, & Discoveries of the English Nation* (1508–1600) (Glasgow, 1903–1905), 10: 447; Walter Raleigh, "The Discoveries of the Large, Rich, and Beautiful Empire of Guiana" in Hakluyt, *The Principal Navigations*, 428.

17. For a brilliant account of the feminization of the New World in the work of Vespucci and Ralegh, see Louise Montrose, "The Work of Gender in the Discourse of Discovery," *Representations* 33 (1991): 1–41.

18. Kolodny, *Lay of the Land*, 9. See chapter 2 for an excellent analysis of early English exploration and colonization, 1500–1740.

19. McClintock, *Imperial Leather*, 24.

20. Ibid.

21. John Smith may have drawn his portrait of Pocahontas from the account of Juan Ortiz who, in 1528, was lost in Florida and was located twelve years later by De Soto. Ortiz was supposedly "captured by Indians, and saved at the last second from burning at the stake by the chief's daughter, who later came at night in peril of her life to warn him of her father's plot to kill him." Smith may have known of this story, which was translated by Hakluyt in 1609. See Philip Young, "The Mother of Us All: Pocahontas Reconsidered," *Kenyon Review* 24 (1962), 394.

22. Gary B. Nash, *Red, White, and Black: The Peoples of Early America* (Englewood Cliffs, N.J.: Prentice-Hall Press, 1974), 66.

23. For more on the conquering of Aztec women, see Julie Nash's "Aztec Women: The Transition from Status to Class in Empire and Colony," in *Women and Colonization: Anthropological Perspectives*, ed. Mona Etienne and Eleanor Leacock (New York: Praeger Press, 1980). Julie Nash notes, "the cliché that the Spanish Conquest was a conquest of women is only half true. On the one hand, women

in the conquered and tribute-paying areas of the Aztec empire had already experienced enslavement and prostitution. On the other hand, since the Spaniards included only a few women—about a tenth of their numbers in the early decades—Indian women became wives and concubines of conquerors and often enjoyed treatment preferential to that of men" (136). Nash ultimately determines that "the half truth that the conquest of the Americas was the conquest of women can be separated in terms of an analytical separation of forms of reproduction. A more accurate statement would be that the conquest was not of women, but of Indian male control over the reproductive power of women, with the result that the Spaniards claimed the right to recruit the children born of their relations with Indian women as heirs of laborers." Most important to this study, patriarchal power "with the male as head of household" was instituted more forcefully through Spanish colonization of the Aztec people (145).

24. Nash, *Red, White, and Black*, 67.

25. Robert S. Tilton, *Pocahontas: The Evolution of An American Narrative* (Cambridge: Cambridge University Press, 1994), 12, 14.

26. Nash, *Red, White, and Black*, 67.

27. I have chosen to draw most of my historical background on Native Americans in this chapter from the Virginia colony and the Algonkians of Coastal North America in the seventeenth century because Virginia was England's first successful colony and because it was the colony most supportive of royalist interests throughout this period. Most of the plays examined in this text reflect both of these concerns—Shakespeare invested in the Virginia Company, and his *Tempest* has been shown repeatedly to draw on Virginia history, and Behn and Dryden were both royalists.

28. Paula Gunn Allen, *The Sacred Hoop: Recovering the Feminine in American Indian Traditions* (Boston: Beacon Press, 1986), 32.

29. Gayatri Chakravorty Spivak, "Can the Subaltern Speak?" in *Marxism and the Interpretation of Literature*, ed. Cary Nelson and Larry Grossberg (Urbana: University of Illinois, 1988), 287. See also Trinh T. Minh-ha, *Woman, Native, Other: Writing Postcoloniality and Feminism* (Bloomington: Indiana University Press, 1989), especially, 64–65. A number of other postcolonial critics argue that the other (male and female) is unknowable. See for example, Edward Said, *Orientalism*, 1–28; Clifford Geertz, "Cerebral Savage: On the Work of Claude Levi-Strauss," in *The Interpretation of Cultures* (New York: Basic Books, 1973), 345–359; Johannes Fabian, *Time and the Other: How Anthropology Makes Its Object* (New York: Columbia University Press, 1983).

30. Allen, *Sacred Hoops*, 3.

31. Robert Steven Grumet, "Sunksquaws, Shamans, and Tradeswomen: Middle Atlantic Coastal Algonkian Women During the 17th and 18th Centuries," *Women and Colonization: Anthropological Perspectives*, ed. Mona Etienne and Eleanor Leacock (New York: Praeger Publishers, 1980), 46.

32. Grumet, "Sunksquaws, Shamans, and Tradeswomen," 50.

33. Ibid., 51.

34. Ibid.

35. Ibid., 52.

36. Ibid., 53, 54.

37. Ibid., 59.

38. Ibid., 46.

39. Kathleen M. Brown, *Gender, Race, and Power in Colonial Virginia: Good Wives, Nasty Wenches, and Anxious Patriarchs* (Chapel Hill: University of North Carolina Press, 1996), 51–52. I am deeply indebted to Brown's groundbreaking historical study of Virginia, which brings together and synthesizes historical documentation on gender, race, and patriarchal power. Her study demonstrates the necessity for examining race and gender in specific historical contexts.

40. Brown, *Gender, Race, and Power*, 53.

41. Ibid., 50.

42. Andrew Gerard Berthelemy, *Black Face, Maligned Race: The Representation of Blacks in English Drama from Shakespeare to Southerne* (Baton Rouge: Louisiana State University Press, 1987). On black women's sexuality, see 123, 124, 133. Barthelemy points out further that the terms "India" or "Indian" meant exotic in generalized terms; Indians could be black or tawny, from the East or West Indies, see 48.

43. Brown, *Gender, Race and Power*, 15.

44. Ibid., 28.

45. Ibid., 26.

46. Ibid., 46.

47. Ibid., 195.

48. *SAL*, April 16, 1691, III. Quoted in Brown, 197.

49. Brown, *Gender, Race, and Power*, 187.

50. Ibid., 41.

51. Ibid., 149.

52. Ibid., 145.

53. Ibid., 115.

54. Ibid., 108.

55. Lynda E. Boose, " 'The Getting of a Lawful Race': Racial Discourse in Early Modern England and the Unrepresentable Black Woman," in *Women, "Race," and Writing in the Early Modern Period*, ed. Margo Hendricks and Patricia Parker (London: Routledge, 1994), 47.

56. Nash, *Red, White, and Black*, 182.

57. Homi K. Bhaba, "Of Mimicry and Man: The Ambivalence of Colonial Discourse," and "Signs Taken for Wonders: Questions of Ambivalence and Authority under a Tree Outside Delhi, May 1817," *The Location of Culture* (London: Routledge Press, 1994), 89, 102–122.

58. Homi K. Bhabha, "The Other Question: Stereotype, Discrimination and the Discourse of Colonialism," *The Location of Culture*, 66.

59. On the theme of the wild man within the Englishman, see Richard Ashcraft, "Leviathan Triumphant: Thomas Hobbes and the Politics of Wild Men," *The Wild Man Within*, 141–181; Earl Miner, "The Wild Man through the Looking Glass," *The Wild Man Within*, 87–114.

60. Roach, *Cities of the Dead*, 3.

61. Ibid., 2.

62. See for example, David McDonald's "Unspeakable Justice: David Hare's Fanshen," who writes that "Difference, within identity, generates the awareness of representation as an image that stands apart from the thing it represents," 129. In *Critical Theory and Performance*, ed. Janelle G. Reinelt and Joseph R. Roach

(Ann Arbour: University of Michigan Press, 1992). Roach argues similarly: "What remains physically present to the spectators in the theater is the natural body of the performer. . . . This dichotomy provokes a constant alternation of attention from actor to role, from vulnerable body to enduring memory, in which, at any moment one or the other ought to be forgotten but cannot be" (82).

63. Timothy Murray, *Theatrical Legitimation: Allegories of Genius in Seventeenth-Century England and France* (New York: Oxford University Press, 1987) 15, 14.

64. Susan J. Owen, *Restoration Theatre and Crisis* (Oxford: Clarendon Press, 1996), 11.

65. Robert Markley, *Two Edg'd Weapons: Style and Ideology in the Comedies of Etherege, Wycherly and Congreve* (Oxford: Clarendon Press, 1988), 26, 27. Markley examines linguistic style and ideology in Restoration comedy, but his argument is relevant here.

66. See Kristina Straub, *Sexual Suspects: Eighteenth-Century Players and Sexual Ideology* (Princeton: Princeton University Press, 1992). Also, Thomas A. King, " 'As If (She) Were Made on Purpose to Put the Whole World into Good Humour': Reconstructing the First English Actresses," *The Drama Review: A Journal of Performance Studies* 36 (Fall 1992): 3, 78–101.

67. See Bhabha, "Of Mimicry and Man" (85–101), "Signs Taken for Wonders" (102–122), "The Other Question" (66–84), *The Location of Culture*.

68. John Locke, *Two Treaties of Government*, ed. Peter Laslett (Cambridge: Cambridge University Press, 1960), 301.

## Chapter One

1. Paul Brown, " 'This Thing of Darkness I Acknowledge Mine': *The Tempest* and the Discourse of Colonialism," in *Political Shakespeare: New Essays in Cultural Materialism*, ed. Jonathan Dollimore and Alan Sinfield (Ithaca: Cornell University Press, 1985), 48.

2. On the female characters in *The Tempest*, see Stephen Orgel's "Prospero's Wife," in *Rewriting the Renaissance: The Discourse of Sexual Difference in Early Modern Europe*, ed. Margaret Ferguson et al. (Chicago: University of Chicago Press, 1986), 50–64; and Ann Thompson, " 'Miranda, Where's Your Sister?': Reading Shakespeare's *The Tempest*," in *Feminist Criticism: Theory and Practise*, ed. Susan Sellers (New York, Harvester Wheatsheaf, 1991). See also, Kim Hall's *Things of Darkness: Economics of Race and Gender in Early Modern England* (Ithaca: Cornell University Press, 1995), 141–153. Hall brings together questions of race and gender in her discussion of Shakespeare's *Tempest* (and she points out rightly that most Shakespeare critics do not).

3. In "Shakespeare and the Cannibals," in *Cannibals, Witches, and Divorce: Estranging the Renaissance*, ed. Marjorie B. Garber (Baltimore: Johns Hopkins University Press, 1987), Stephen Orgel argues that Prospero's "vision" expresses "how deeply the fears for Miranda's chastity are implicated with his sense of his own power" (65).

4. For an excellent account of the politics in Shakespeare's *Tempest* and their difference in Dryden's and Davenant's 1667 *Enchanted Island*, see Katherine Eisaman Maus, "Arcadia Lost: Politics and Revision in the Restoration *Tempest*," ed. Mary Beth Rose, *Renaissance Drama as Cultural History: Essays From Renais-*

*sance Drama 1977–1987* (Evanston, Ill.: Northwestern University Press, 1990), especially 139–140. See also Michael Neill, "Heroic Heads and Humble Tails: Sex, Politics, and the Restoration Comic Rake," *The Eighteenth Century* 24 (1983): 115–139, for an important account of the relationship of Restoration politics and drama.

5. Laura Brown, *Ends of Empire: Women and Ideology in Early Eighteenth-Century English Literature* (Ithaca: Cornell University Press), especially chapters 2, 4, 6.

6. In his "Commentary" to *The Enchanted Island*, in *The Works of John Dryden*, ed. Maximillian Novak et al. (Berkeley: University of California Press, 1970), Maximillian Novak notes that in November 1667 when Clarendon was about to be removed from office, Samuel Pepys and the royal court took time out to see the operatic version of *The Enchanted Island* at the Duke's Company at Lincoln's Inn Fields. Pepys saw the play seven times (319). It was performed for royalty four times (322). Dryden's and Davenant's *Tempest, or The Enchanted Island* will hereafter be referred to as *The Enchanted Island*.

7. *The Sea Voyage* opened five weeks before Davenant's and Dryden's *Tempest* at the King's Company in 1667 (Novak, "Commentary," 320).

8. George Robert Guffey, *After the Tempest* (Los Angeles: University of California, 1969), ix.

9. Guffey, *After the Tempest*, xv.

10. There a few exceptions: Michael Dobson's chapters 1 and 2, in *The Making of the National Poet: Shakespeare, Adaptation and Authorship, 1660–1769* (Oxford: Clarendon Press, 1995)—Dobson discusses gender at length in his work on *The Tempests*, but he does not consider race; Maus's "Arcadia Lost"—Maus astutely examines the politics in Dryden's and Davenant's *Tempest*, but she does not include the significance of race or gender in her analysis; and Guffey, *After the Tempest*.

For new historical and theoretical readings of Shakespeare's *Tempest*, see, for example, Meredith Ann Skura, "Discourse and the Individual: The Case of Colonialism in *The Tempest*," *Shakespeare Quarterly* 40 (Spring 1989): 42–69; Stephen Greenblatt, "Learning to Curse: Aspects of Linguistic Colonialism in the Sixteenth Century" in Modern Critical Interpretations: *William Shakespeare's The Tempest*, ed. Harold Bloom (New York: Chelsea House, 1988), 65–67; Peter Hulme, "Hurricanes in the Caribbees: The Constitution of the Discourse of English Colonialism" in *1642: Literature and Power in the Seventeenth Century, Proceedings of the Essex conference on the Sociology of Literature*, ed. Francis Barker et al. (Colchester: University of Essex, 1981), 55–83; Peter Hulme, *Colonial Encounters: Europe and the Native Caribbean, 1492–1797* (London: Methuen, 1986), 89–134; Francis Barker and Peter Hulme, "Nymphs and Reapers Heavily Vanish: The Discursive Contexts of The Tempest," in *Alternative Shakespeares*, ed. John Drakakis (London: Methuen, 1985), 191–205; Brown, "This Thing of Darkness' "; Orgel, "Prospero's Wife"; Orgel, "Shakespeare and the Cannibals"; Mary Loeffelholz, "Miranda in the New World: *The Tempest* and Charlotte Barnes's *The Forest Princess*," in *Women's Re-Visions of Shakespeare: On the Response of Dickinson, Woolf, Rich, H. D., George Eliot, and Others*, ed. Marianne Novy (Urbana: University of Illinois Press, 1990), 58–75; the final chapter of Ania Loomba's, *Gender, Race, Renaissance Drama* (Manchester: Manchester University Press, 1989), pp. 142–158; and Kim Hall's *Things of Darkness*, 141–153.

11. *The New Eighteenth Century: Theory, Politics, English Literature*, ed. Felicity Nussbaum and Laura Brown (New York: Methuen Press, 1987), 1, 13; Brown, *Ends of Empire*; Hall, *Things of Darkness; Cultural Readings of Restoration and Eighteenth-Century English Theater*, ed. J. Douglas Canfield and Deborah C. Payne (Athens, Ga.: University of Georgia Press, 1995); *Women, "Race," and Writing*, ed. Hendricks and Parker; Srinivas Aravamudan, *Tropicopolitans: Colonialism and Agency, 1699–1804* (Durham, N.C.: Duke University Press, 1999).

12. George Guffey, "Politics, Weather, and the Contemporary Reception of the Dryden-Davenant *Tempest*," *Restoration* 8 (1984): 1–9; Earl Miner "The Wild Man in the Looking Glass," in *The Wild Man Within: An Image in Western Thought from Renaissance to Romanticism*, ed. Dudley Moore and Maximillian Novak (Pittsburgh: University of Pittsburgh, 1972); Novak, "Commentary" to Dryden's and Davenant's *Enchanted Island*, 332; and Maus, "Arcadia Lost."

13. Gayatri Chakravorty Spivak, "Three Women's Texts and a Critique of Imperialism," in *"Race," Writing, and Difference*, ed. Henry Louis Gates, Jr. (Chicago: University of Chicago Press, 1986), 262.

14. See Robert S. Tilton, *Pocahontas: The Evolution of An American Narrative* (Cambridge: Cambridge University Press, 1994), chapter 1, for an excellent description of contemporary views of miscegenation in the Pocahontas myth in the early colonial era.

15. Rayna Green, "The Pocahontas Perplex: The Image of Indian Women in American Culture," *Massachusetts Review* 16 (1975): 702–703. Green explains what happens to the image of the native woman when the colonies seek and achieve independence; the focus of her article in on nineteenth-century American literature, yet her point about the split view of the native woman is pertinent to my study of the seventeenth century.

For other analyses of the Pocahontas myth in American literature, see Leslie A. Fiedler, *The Return of the Vanishing American* (New York: Stein and Day, 1968), 84–108; Asebrit Sundquist, *Pocahontas & Co.: The Fictional American Indian Woman in Nineteenth-Century Literature: A Study of Method* (New Jersey: Humanities Press International, 1987); Mary V. Dearborn, *Pocahontas's Daughters: Gender and Ethnicity in American Culture* (New York: Oxford University Press, 1986).

On the Pocahontas myth and colonial discourse, see also, Peter Hulme's astute analysis in *Colonial Encounters*, chapter 4.

16. The act that has made our heroine so famous—laying her head across John Smith's in order to save him from her father's blows—is the point at which historians most actively question the truth of her tale. The debate goes as follows: Pocahontas's saving John Smith's life at the hazard of her own was not recorded in Smith's *True Relation* of 1608, which describes his capture by Powhatan. Nor is Pocahontas's act recorded by anyone else in the colony until 1622, when Smith reports that Pocahontas saved him in his *New England Trials*. The story was included in Smith's *Generall Historie* which was published in 1624. See Philip Young, "The Mother of Us All: Pocahontas Reconsidered," *Kenyon Review* 24 (1962), 397. As a result of Smith's delays in recording the event (and of his being the only white witness to the incident), historians argue over whether Pocahontas's preservation of Smith occurred; some contend that the event may have been added to Smith's *Generall Historie* simply for dramatic effect. See the footnote to John Smith's account in *The Generall Historie of Virginia, New England, and the*

*Summer Isles*, in *The Complete Works of John Smith (1580–1631)*, ed. Philip Barbour (Chapel Hill: University of North Carolina Press, 1986), 2: 146; and the footnote to William Strachey's *Historie of Travaile into Virginia Britannia*, ed. Louis B. Wright and Virginia Freund (Great Britain: University of Glasgow, 1953), 72. (Originally printed 1615.)

See also J. A. Leo Lemay's *Did Pocahontas Save Captain John Smith?* (Athens, Ga.: University of Georgia Press, 1992), in which he covers the debate and argues that Pocahontas did save Smith.

17. Robert Beverley, *The History and Present State of Virginia* (1705), ed. Louis B. Wright (Chapel Hill: University of North Carolina Press, 1947), 28.

18. Ralph Hamor, *A True Discourse of the Present State of Virginia* (London: Printed for John Beale for William Welby, 1615; reprint, Richmond: Virginia State Press, 1957, intro. A. L. Rowse), 11.

19. Hamor, *A True Discourse*, 11–12.

20. Ibid., 15.

21. Barbour, Philip L., *Pocahontas and Her World* (Boston: Houghton Mifflin, 1970), 131.

22. Strachey, *Historie of Travaile*, 62.

23. Barbour, *Pocahontas*, 99 and 264n1.

24. Karen Ordahl Kupperman, *Settling with the Indians: The Meeting of English and Indian Cultures in America, 1580–1640* (New Jersey: Roman and Littlefield, 1975), 18.

25. William Warren Jenkins, "The Princess Pocahontas and Three Englishmen Named John," *No Fairer Land: Studies in Southern Literature before 1900*, ed. J. Lasley Dameron and James W. Mathews (New York: Whitston Publishing, 1986), 11.

26. Young, "The Mother of Us All," 393.

27. Hulme, *Colonial Encounters*, 143.

28. Tilton States, "interpreters of the Pocahontas narrative, out of respect for her actions as well as her royal status, consistently felt this need to celebrate her family and thereby segregate it from the offspring of other similar but less 'noble' unions," 18.

29. Quoted in Grace Steele Woodward, *Pocahontas* (Norman: University of Oklahoma Press, 1963), 87.

30. Joseph Roach, *Cities of the Dead: Circum-Atlantic Performance* (New York: Columbia University Press, 1996), 122.

31. Smith, *Generall Historie*, 298–299.

32. Hulme, *Colonial Encounters*, 143.

33. Smith, *Generall Historie*, 128.

34. Warren M. Billings, ed., *The Old Dominion in the Seventeenth Century: A Documentary History of Virginia, 1609–1689* (Chapel Hill: University of North Carolina Press, 1975), 7.

35. This shipwreck may have inspired Shakespeare's *Tempest*, as Miner (as well as many others) points out in *Wild Man*, 95.

36. Quoted in Billings, *The Old Dominion*.

37. Quoted in Barbour, Pocahontas, 65. When his crime was discovered, this man was burned alive; his confession was forced from him while he hung by his thumbs.

38. Billings, *The Old Dominion*, 7.

39. Smith, "Capt. Smith's PETITION to her Majesty, in Behalf of Pocahontas, Daughter to the Indian Emperor Powhatan," in Robert Beverley, *The History and Present State of Virginia*, ed. Louis B. Wright (1705; reprint, Chapel Hill: University of North Carolina Press, 1947), 41.

40. Smith, "Capt. Smith's PETITION," 42.

41. Strachey portrays the Virginia Native American women in general as promiscuous and sexually wild: if the husband of a native woman allows it, he writes, she "may embrace the acquaintance of any Straunger for nothing, and yt is accompted no offense and incredible yt is, with what heat both sexes of them are given over to those intemperances." Because of the women's promiscuity, they are given to contracting venereal disease "very young." (Strachey, *History of Travaile*, 113.)

42. Smith, *Generall Historie*, 182–183.

43. On the problematic of the male and female gaze in film, see Laura Mulvey, "Visual Pleasure and Narrative Cinema," *Screen* 16 (1975): 6–18; Laura Mulvey, "On Duel in the Sun," *Framework* 15–17 (1981): 12–15; Mary Ann Doane, "Film and Masquerade: Theorising the Female Spectator," *Screen* 23 (1982): 74–88.

44. Robert J. C. Young, *Colonial Desire: Hybridity in Theory, Culture, and Race* (London: Routledge Press, 1995), 19.

45. Woodward, *Pocahontas*, 57, emphasis added.

46. Barbour, *Pocahontas*, 111.

47. Thomas Dale, "To the R. and My Most Esteemed *Friend Mr. D. M. at His House at F. Ch. in London*." Reprinted in Hamor, *True Discourse*, 55–56. (Originally written in 1614.)

48. Alexander Whitaker, "To My Verie Deere and Loving Cosen M. G. Minister of the B. F. in London" (1614). Reprinted in Hamor, *True Discourse*, 59–60.

49. John Rolfe, "The Letter to Sir Thomas Dale." Reprinted in Hamor, *True Discourse*, 63.

50. Beverley, *History and Present State*, 38–39.

51. Susan J. Owen, *Restoration Theatre and Crisis* (Oxford: Clarendon Press, 1996), 10. In this study, Owen argues persuasively about the contradictory nature of patriarchal ideology throughout the Restoration and in the drama of the period, see especially chapters 1 and 2.

52. In "Prospero's Wife," Orgel suggests that the instability of royal authority in the early seventeenth century stemmed from questions of female inheritance (59).

53. William Shakespeare, *The Tempest*, ed. Robert Langbaum (New York: Signet Classic, 1987). All further references will be from this edition; line and page numbers will appear in the text.

54. In *Colonial Encounters*, Hulme argues that, "there is a precise match with the situation of Europeans in American during the seventeenth century, whose technology (especially of firearms) suddenly became magical when introduced into a less technologically developed society, but who were incapable (for a variety of reasons) of feeding themselves" (128). John Smith, for example, while in search of food for the Virginia settlement, was caught by a group of Indians and nearly killed, but he saved himself by showing his captors his compass. The Indian King

Opencanaugh was so impressed with the instrument that he decided to let Smith live. See Smith, *The Generall Historie*, 146–147. Stephen Greenblatt also notes that Columbus used his knowledge of an imminent eclipse to frighten the natives and force them to submit. See "Invisible Bullets: Renaissance Authority and Its Subversion, *Henry IV and Henry V*," ed. Jonathan Dollimore and Alan Sinfield, *Political Shakespeare: New Essays in Cultural Materialism* (Ithaca: Cornell University Press, 1985), 18–47.

55. Michael Adas, *Machines as the Measure of Men: Science, Technology, and Ideologies of Western Dominance* (Ithaca: Cornell University Press, 1989), 33. On technology and imperialism, see also, Bruno Latour, trans. Catherine Porter, *We Have Never Been Modern* (Cambridge, Mass.: Harvard University Press, 1993), and Alfred W. Crosby, *Ecological Imperialism: The Biological Expansion of Europe, 900–1900.* (Cambridge: Cambridge University Press, 1986).

56. Orgel, "Prospero's Wife," 54.

57. Sycorax, as Novak notes in regard to Dryden's and Davenant's adaptation of Shakespeare's play, is "made to embody all the sensuality that Western man has imagined to be characteristic of women of dark-skinned races. By 1668, polygamous, polyandrous, and even incestuous societies had been discovered by voyagers, and Sycorax is a typically libertine object lesson in the conventional and regional nature of monogamy. Sycorax is interested solely in sex, whether with Trinculo, his subjects, or her own brother" ("Commentary," 335).

58. As Brown argues in "This Thing of Darkness," "the other is here presented to legitimate the seizure of power by civility and to define by antithesis (rape) the proper course of civil courtship—a channeling of desire into a series of formal tasks and maneuvers and, finally, into courtly marriage" (63). Laura E. Donaldson points out that Caliban has been seen by critics solely as a displaced colonized subject, but in her view, though he participates in the violent assertion of male dominance over women through the attempted rape of Miranda, Caliban cannot see how Prospero dominates both of them. Thus, "trapped in this vicious paradox, Caliban reinforces, rather than weakens, the chains of their mutual enslavement" (16–17). In *Decolonizing Feminisms: Race, Gender, and Empire Building* (Chapel Hill: University of North Carolina Press, 1992).

59. See Barker and Hulme, "Nymphs and Reapers," in which they argue that in the "reconciliation" of Italian nobility, the threat of the New World is revealed (203).

60. Barker and Hulme argue that Prospero's disavowal of Caliban's claim to the island is a "characteristic trope by which European colonial regimes articulated their authority over land to which they could have no conceivable legitimate claim" ("Nymphs and Reapers," 200).

61. C. E. Carrington, *The British Overseas: Exploits of a Nation of Shopkeepers* (Cambridge: Cambridge University Press, 1950), 54. See also Francis Jennings, *The Invasion of America: Indians, Colonialism, and the Cant of Conquest* (Chapel Hill: University of North Carolina Press, 1975), 37.

62. Hulme, *Hurricane*, 99. See also Billings, *The Old Dominion*, 207. For a detailed analysis of the stereotype of the Indian, see Robert F. Berkhofer, Jr., *The White Man's Indian: Images of the American Indian from Columbus to the Present* (New York: Knopf, 1978).

63. Kathleen M. Brown, *Good Wives, Nasty Wenches, Anxious Patriarchs: Gender, Race, and Power in Colonial Virginia* (Chapel Hill: University of North Carolina, 1996), 187.

64. Andrew Barthelemy points out that Indians and blacks were portrayed interchangeably in the seventeenth-century literature—they were depicted as "exotic" in "generalized" terms. In *Black Face, Maligned Race: The Representation of Blacks in English Drama from Shakespeare to Southerne* (Baton Rouge: Louisiana State University Press, 1987), 48.

65. Historically, European colonists expected the natives to serve them, and when they did not, Europeans portrayed the natives as menacing and evil. Greenblatt, "Invisible Bullets," 29–30.

66. John Fletcher, *The Sea-Voyage, in The Works of Francis Beaumont and John Fletcher*, vol. 9, ed. A. R. Waller (Cambridge: Cambridge University Press, 1910). All citations will be from this edition; line and page numbers will be cited in the text.

67. Christopher Columbus, *The Four Voyages of Christopher Columbus*, ed. and trans. J. M. Cohen (London: Penguin, 1969), 98.

68. Sir Walter Ralegh Knight, *The Discovery of the Large, Rich, and Beuutiful Empyre of Guiana* (Imprinted London: Robert Robinson, 1596), 23–24.

69. Columbus, *Voyages*, 196–197.

70. Greenblatt, *Marvelous Possessions: The Wonder of the World* (Chicago: University of Chicago Press, 1991), 81.

71. Diane Dugaw, *Warrior Women and Popular Balladry, 1650–1850* (Cambridge: Cambridge University Press, 1989), 144, 143.

72. For other useful work on Amazons, see Page duBois, *Centaurs and Amazons: Women and the Pre-History of the Great Chain of Being* (Ann Arbor: University of Michigan Press, 1982); Abby Wetten Kleinbaum, *The War Against Amazons* (New York: McGraw-Hill, 1983); Sharon W. Tiffany and Kathleen J. Adams, *The Wild Woman: An Inquiry into the Anthropology of an Idea* (Cambridge, Mass.: Schenkman Publishing, 1985); William Blake Tyrrel, *Amazons: A Study in Athenian Mythmaking* (Baltimore: Johns Hopkins Press, 1984); Julie Wheelwright, *Amazons and Military Maids* (London: Pandora Press, 1989); Simon Shephard, *Amazons and Warrior Women in Seventeenth-Century Drama* (New York: St. Martin's Press, 1981); Stephen Orgel, "Jonson and the Amazons," in *Soliciting Interpretation: Literary Theory and Seventeenth-Century English Poetry*, ed. Elizabeth D. Harvey and Katherine Eisamen Maus (Chicago: University Press of Chicago, 1990), pp. 119–139; Kim Hall, *Things of Darkness*, 43.

Chapter Two

1. See George Guffey, "Politics, Weather, and the Contemporary Reception of the Dryden-Davenant *Tempest*," *Restoration* 8 (1984): 1–9, for a fascinating account of the way Dryden's and Davenant's revisions include political relations between Spain, France, and England.

2. Guffey, "Politics, Weather," 2.

3. Katherine Eisaman Maus, "Arcadia Lost: Politics and Revision in the Restoration *Tempest*," ed. Mary Beth Rose, *Renaissance Drama as Cultural History:*

*Essays From Renaissance Drama 1977–1987* (Evanston: Northwestern University Press, 1990), 202.

4. Michael Neill, "Heroic Heads and Humble Tails: Sex, Politics, and the Restoration Comic Rake," *The Eighteenth Century* 24 (1983): 118, 116.

5. Susan Staves, *Players' Scepters: Fictions of Authority in the Restoration* (Lincoln: University of Nebraska Press, 1979), 41.

6. Linda Colley, *Britons: Forging the Nation 1707–1837* (New Haven: Yale University Press, 1992), 5.

7. Christopher Hill, *The Century of Revolution 1603–1714* (1961; reprint, New York: Norton, 1982), 209.

8. David Hawke, *The Colonial Experience* (Indianapolis: Bobbs-Merrill, 1966), 193.

9. Hill, *Century*, 211.

10. See Colley, *Britons*. Michael McKeon argues that the general sentiment prevailed that the means to English "prosperity was the national balance of trade." It was believed that if exports exceeded imports that would constitute "monetary profit for all." (*The Politics and Poetics of Restoration England: The Case of Dryden's "Annus Mirabilis"* [Cambridge: Harvard University Press, 1975]), 101.

11. See Novak's "Commentary" to *The Enchanted Island*, in *The Works of John Dryden*, vol. 10, ed. Maximillian Novak et al. (Berkeley: University of California Press, 1970). An operatic version of the play, brought out by Thomas Shadwell, appeared in 1674. The 1674 revision differs only slightly from the 1670 text; some of the text has been cut, and dancing and music were added which "transformed" the play into "a colossally successful, spectacular dramatic opera" (322). My reading of the play will refer to the 1667 version.

12. Michael Dobson, *The Making of a National Poet: Shakespeare, Adaptation and Authorship, 1660–1769* (Oxford: Clarendon Press, 1995), 54–56. Significantly, Dobson notes that Moll Davis became one of Charles II's mistresses within one month of the premiere of *The Enchanted Island* (56). This creates interesting ideological links between female prostitution and the English crown.

13. Earl Miner "The Wild Man in the Looking Glass," in *The Wild Man Within: An Image in Western Thought from Renaissance to Romanticism*, ed. Dudley Moore and Maximillian Novak (Pittsburgh: University of Pittsburgh, 1972), 104.

14. In his "Introduction" to *After the Tempest* (Los Angeles: University of California Press, 1969), George Guffey points out that the "Prospero of the later play is a considerably weaker figure than the earlier Shakespeare character; his lack of control over the destiny of the lovers almost leads to tragedy, rather than tragicomedy" (viii–ix). See also Eckhard Auberlen, "The Tempest and the Concerns of Restoration Court: A Study of *The Enchanted Island* and the Operatic *Tempest*," *Restoration* 15 (1991): 71–88, for a similar critique of Prospero's loss of power in this adaptation.

15. *The Enchanted Island* in *The Works of John Dryden*, vol. 10, ed. H. T. Swedenberg et al. (Berkeley: *University of California Press*, 1970). All citations are from this edition; line and page numbers will be cited in the text.

16. As Maus points out in "Arcadia Lost," "the ideological basis of [Prospero's] authority is subverted by the possibility that the patriarchal conception of monarchy is bankrupt" (142).

17. Dobson, *Making of a National Poet*, 56.

18. See Marjorie Garbor, *Vested Interests: Cross-Dressing and Cultural Anxiety* (New York: Routledge Press, 1992). Garbor argues that cross-dressing causes and marks "category cris[e]s" and "displacements from the axis of *class* as well as from *race* onto the axis of gender," 17.

19. Miner "Wild Man," 104.

20. Thomas Duffett, *The Mock-Tempest: or the Enchanted Castle* (London: William Cadman, 1675). All citations are from this edition; line and page numbers will be cited in the text.

21. C. E. Carrington, *The British Overseas: Exploits of a Nation of Shopkeepers* (Cambridge: Cambridge University Press, 1950), 44.

22. In *Century*, Hill points outs that merchant shipping doubled between 1660 and 1668, and by 1686, "forty percent of English ships were engaged in trade with America and India. The Acts created monopoly conditions of trade with the colonies, and so increased . . . Charles II's authority. . . . They mark a decisive turning point in England's economic history" (211).

23. See McKeon, *Politics and Poetry*, 80–81.

24. In *Ends of Empire: Women and Ideology in Early Eighteenth-Century English Literature* (Ithaca: Cornell University Press, 1993), Laura Brown suggests that English women bear responsibility for the commodification of English culture.

25. Neill, "Heroic Heads," 117.

26. Thomas Durfey, *A Common-Wealth of Women* (London: R. Bentley, 1686). All references are to this edition; page and line numbers will be cited in the text.

Chapter Three

1. See Michael McKeon, *The Politics and Poetics of Restoration England: The Case of Dryden's "Annus Mirabilis"* (Cambridge: Harvard University Press, 1975), 101. See also Andrew B. Appleby's *Famine in Tudor and Stuart England* (Stanford: Stanford University Press, 1978).

2. Cortes is spelled in the same manner throughout this chapter.

3. James Anderson Winn, *"When Beauty Fires the Blood": Love and the Arts in the Age of Dryden* (Ann Arbor: University of Michigan Press, 1992), 67–69.

4. Jacqueline Pearson, *The Prostituted Muse: Images of Women & Women Dramatists 1642–1737* (New York: St. Martin's Press, 1988), 47.

5. Joseph Roach, "The Artificial Eye: Augustan Theater and the Empire of the Visible," in *Performance of Power: Theatrical Discourse and Politics*, ed. Sue-Ellen Case and Janelle Reinelt (Iowa City: University of Iowa Press, 1991), 131–145, and his more recent *Cities of the Dead: Circum-Atlantic Performance* (New York: Columbia University Press, 1996), especially pages 122–178.

6. For an important reading of colonialism and *The Indian Queen and Indian Emperour*, see Bridget Orr's *Empire on the English Stage, 1660–1714* (Cambridge: Cambridge University Press, forthcoming). Orr's analysis is not primarily concerned with gender, however. For other varied and useful readings of *The Indian Queen* and *The Indian Emperour* (but, which dismiss or ignore the crucial connections among gender and race, and the justification for colonial oppression in these plays), see Anne T. Barbeau, *The Intellectual Design of John Dryden's Heroic Plays* (New Haven: Yale University Press, 1970); Derek Hughes, *Dryden's Heroic Plays* (Lincoln: University of Nebraska Press, 1981), 22–58; John Loftis, *The Spanish*

*Plays of Neoclassical England* (New Haven: Yale University Press, 1973); John Loftis, "Commentary to *The Indian Emperour*" in *The Works of John Dryden*, vol. 9, ed. H. T. Swedenberg, Jr. et al. (Berkeley: University of California Press, 1966); John A. Winterbottom, "The Place of Hobbesian Ideas in Dryden's Tragedies," *Journal of English and Germanic Philology* 57 (1958): 665–683; Max Harris, "Aztec Maidens in Satin Gowns: *Alterity and Dialogy* in Dryden's *Indian Emperour* and Hogarth's *The Conquest of Mexico*," *Restoration* 15 (1991): 59–70; Michael M. Alssid, *Dryden's Rhymed Heroic Tragedies* (Salzburg: Institut fur Englische Sprache and literatur, 1974); David R. Evans, " 'Private Greatness': The Feminine Ideal in Dryden's Early Heroic Drama," *Restoration* 16 (1992): 2–19; David Bruce Kramer, "Onely Victory in Him: The Imperial Dryden," in *The Imperial Dryden: The Poetics of Appropriation in Seventeenth-Century England* (Athens: University of Georgia Press, 1994), 63–115; J. M. Armistead, "Dryden and the Popular Tradition: Backgrounds for *King Arthur* and *The Indian Emperour*," in *Notes and Queries* 31 (1984): 342–44.

7. Cherrie Moraga, "From a Long Line of Vendidas: Chicanas and Feminism," *Feminist Studies, Critical Studies*, ed. Teresa de Lauretis (Bloomington: Indiana University Press, 1986), 174–175.

8. Stephen Greenblatt, *Marvelous Possessions: The Wonder of the New World*, (Chicago: University of Chicago Press, 1991), 143. See also Tzetan Todorov's analysis of Marina/Malinche, in *The Conquest of America: The Question of the Other*, trans. Richard Howard (New York: Harper and Row, 1982), 100–101.

9. Bernal Diaz del Castillo, *The Discovery and Conquest of Mexico 1517–1521*, ed. Genero Garcia, trans. A. P. Maudslay (New York: Ferrar, Strauss, Cudahy, 1956), 66. See also Francisco Lopez de Gomara, *Cortes: The Life of the Conqueror by His Secretary*, ed. and trans. Lesley Byrd Simpson (Berkeley: University of California Press, 1964), 56.

10. Diaz, *Discovery and Conquest*, 68.

11. Ibid., 66–67.

12. Lopez, *Cortes*, 48.

13. Diaz, *Discovery and Conquest*, 62–63.

14. Ibid., 67.

15. Ibid., 67–68.

16. Ibid., 174.

17. Lopez, *Cortes*, 127.

18. *Cruelty* and *Sir Francis Drake* were first performed independently of one another during the Interregnum, and they later were incorporated into *A Playhouse to be Let* which was produced in 1663.

19. "Commentary" to *The Indian Emperour*, 309.

20. "Introductory Notice," *The Playhouse To Be Let*, in *The Dramatic Works of Sir William Davenant* (Edinburgh: William Paterson; London: H. Sotheran, 1813), 4:4–5. In his dedication to Cromwell, Phillips wrote, "you are not now to fight against your Country-men, but against your Old and Constant Enemies, the SPANIARDS, a Proud, Deceitful, Cruel, and Treacherous Nation." Quoted in Philip Bordinat and Sophia B. Blaydes, *Sir William Davenant* (Boston: G. K. Hall, 1981), 120.

21. Cromwell's Western Design consisted of an alliance of the Protestant nations and a plan for England to attack Spanish colonies in America. Part of his plan included an attack upon Hispaniola in 1654. Though the raid upon Hispaniola

was unsuccessful, England did acquire Jamaica. Notably, Charles II followed in Cromwell's footsteps by entering into an alliance with Portugal. Prior to the Interregnum, the Portuguese dominions had been joined with those of Spain so that the majority of the New World was held by Spain and Portugal. During the civil war, the Portuguese dominions were no longer incorporated into those of the Spanish, and Portugal entered into a treaty with England. This alliance was solidified with Charles II's marriage to the Portuguese princess, whose dowry brought England Bombay and Tangier. C. E. Carrington, *The British Overseas: Exploits of a Nation of Shopkeepers* (Cambridge: Cambridge University Press, 1950) 45, 46.

22. David Erick Hoegberg, "Colonial Dramas: The Literature of Cultural Interaction Form Davenant to Defoe" (Ph.D. diss., University of Michigan, 1989), 65.

23. Sir William Davenant, *The Cruelty of the Spanish in Peru*, in *The Dramatic Works of William D'Avenant*, vol. 4 (Edinburgh: William Paterson; London: H. Sotheran, 1813). All references will be to this edition; line and page numbers will be cited in the text.

24. Hoegberg, "Colonial Dramas," 73.

25. K. R. Andrews, "The English in the Caribbean, 1560–1620," in ed. K. R. Andrews et al., *The Westward Enterprise: English Activities in Ireland, The Atlantic, and America 1480–1650* (Liverpool: Liverpool University Press, 1978), 113.

26. Sir William Davenant, *The History of Sir Francis Drake, in The Playhouse To Be Let, The Dramatic Works of William D'Avenant*, vol. 4 (Edinburgh: William Paterson; London: H. Sotheran, 1813). All references will be from this edition; page and line numbers will be cited in the text.

27. Frantz Fanon, *Black Skin, White Masks*, trans. Charles Lam Markhamm (New York: Grove Weidenfeld, 1967), 170. As Barthelemy also argues in his discussion of the play, "black men, no matter how noble they may otherwise be, pose a real danger to the community, a danger that always seems to be effected sexually," in *Black Face, Maligned Race*, 173.

28. In "Aztec Maidens in Satin Gowns," Harris suggests that Dryden's recognition that "the European viewpoint is no more privileged than that of the Indian. . . . Faintly 'heralds,' . . . the 'perspectivism' that characterizes our own age" (63). If we are weighing the old world against the new without regard to the female native I might agree; but the native women, in my reading, are not treated as different from, though equal to, the Spaniards (61–62).

29. Harris, "Aztec Maidens," 65. See also Michael M. Alssid's critique of Dryden's inability to see any substantial difference between the Indian and European cultures, in *Dryden's Rhymed Heroic Tragedies*, 143. Orr makes a similar claim, see her *Empire on the English Stage* (forthcoming).

30. Orr, *Empire on the English State* (forthcoming).

31. Loftis, *Spanish Plays*, 38–39.

32. Ibid., 35.

33. Roach, *Cities of the Dead*, 122.

34. John Dryden, *Astraea Redux*, in *John Dryden*, ed. Keith Walker (Oxford University Press, 1987). All references will be to this edition; line numbers will be cited in the text.

35. Roach, *Cities of the Dead*, 2–3.

36. John Dryden and Robert Howard, *The Indian Queen, The Works of John Dryden*, vol. 8, ed. John Harrington Smith et al. (Berkeley: University of California Press, 1962). All references will be to this edition; line and page numbers will be cited in the text.

37. John Dryden, *The Indian Emperour, The Works of John Dryden*, vol. 9, ed. John Loftis et al. (Berkeley: University of California Press, 1966). All references will be to this edition; line and page numbers will be cited in the text.

38. Fray Benardino de Sahagun, *The Conquest of New Spain: 1585 Revision*, ed. S. L. Cline and trans. Howard F. Cline (Salt Lake City: University of Utah Press, 1989), 48.

39. Winterbottom, "The Place of Hobbesian Ideas," 668.


Chapter Four

1. In the 1997 Norton Critical Edition of *Oroonoko*, Joanna Lipking cities thirty-five critical studies of the novel since 1975, and this list is not complete. Catherine Gallagher's critical edition of *Oroonoko* (Boston: Bedford Press, 2000) is a new and very important addition to this list.

2. Srinivas Aravamudan, *Tropicopolitans: Colonialism and Agency, 1688–1804* (Durham: Duke University Press, 1999), 29.

3. Margaret Ferguson, "News from the New World: Miscegenous Romance in Aphra Behn's *Oroonoko* and *The Widow Ranter*" in *The Production of English Renaissance Culture*, ed. David Lee Miller (Ithaca: Cornell University Press, 1994), 151–189; Margo Hendricks, "Civility, Barbarism, and Aphra Behn's *The Widow Ranter*," in *Women, "Race," & Writing in the Early Modern Period*, ed. Margo Hendricks and Patricia Parker (London: Routledge, 1994), 225–239; Jacqueline Pearson, "Slave Princes and Lady Monsters: Gender and Ethnic Difference in the Work of Aphra Behn," in *Aphra Behn Studies*, ed. Janet Todd (Cambridge: Cambridge University Press, 1996), 219–234; Janet Todd, *The Secret Life of Aphra Behn* (London: Andre Deutsch, 1996), chapter 29; Joseph Roach, *Cities of the Dead: Circum-Atlantic Performance* (New York: Columbia University Press, 1996), 122–130. See also Janet Todd, "Spectacular Deaths: History and Story in Aphra Behn's *Love Letters, Oroonoko*, and *The Widow Ranter*," *Gender, Art, and Death* (Cambridge: Cambridge University Press, 1993), 32–62. *The Widow Ranter* is available now in paperback, in *Oroonoko, The Rover, and Other Works*, ed. Janet Todd (London: Penguin Books, 1992).

4. Bridget Orr, *Empire on the English Stage*, 1660–1714 (Cambridge: Cambridge University Press, forthcoming).

5. Ibid.

6. On the problematic of Behn's identity and female authorship, see for example, Catherine Gallagher, "Who Was That Masked Woman? The Prostitute and the Playwright in the Comedies of Aphra Behn," in *Rereading Aphra Behn: History, Theory, Criticism*, ed. Heidi Hutner (Charlottesville: University Press of Virginia, 1993), 65–85; Catherine Gallagher, *Nobody's Story: The Vanishing Acts of Women Writers in the Marketplace, 1670–1820* (Berkeley: University of California Press, 1994); Jessica Munns, " 'Good, Sweet, Honey, Sugar-Candied Reader': Aphra Behn's Foreplay in Forwards," in ed. Hutner, *Rereading Aphra Behn*, 44–62; Janet Todd, *The Sign of Angellica: Women, Writing and Fiction, 1660–1800* (New York:

Columbia University Press, 1989), especially chapters 2 and 4; Moira Ferguson, *Subject to Others: British Women Writers and Colonial Slavery, 1670–1834* (New York: Routledge Press, 1992), chapter 2; Ferguson, "News from the New World," 154. All of her biographers—Maureen Duffy, Angeline Goreau, Janet Todd, among others—comment on it. This list is by no mean exhaustive.

7. Ferguson, "News from the New World," 154.

8. Ferguson, "News from the New World," 181, 188. Charlotte Sussman argues that the narrator effaces Imoinda, in Heidi Hutner ed. *Rereading Aphra Behn*, 228–231; Firdous Azim makes a similar claim, see her *The Colonial Rise of the Novel* (London: Routledge Press, 1993), 51, 60. Aravamudan points out how the efface-ment of Imoinda by her female narrator poses a problem for critics of *Oroonoko* who want to see Behn as an advocate of "progressive ideology, feminism, and empathy for slaves," in *Tropicopolitans*, 31–32.

9. Hendricks, "Civility, Barbarism," 238.

10. Ibid., 227.

11. Roach, *Cities of the Dead*, 122.

12. Robert Markley, " 'Be impudent, be saucy, forward, bold, touzing, and leud': The Politics of Masculine Sexuality and Feminine Desire in Behn's Tory Comedies," in J. Douglas Canfield and Deborah C. Payne, *Cultural Readings of Restoration and Eighteenth-Century Literature* (Athens: University of Georgia Press), 114–140.

13. Heidi Hutner, "Revisioning the Female Body: Aphra Behn's *The Rover, parts, I and II*, in *Rereading Aphra Behn: History, Theory, and Criticism*, ed. Heidi Hutner (Charlottesville: University Press of Virginia, 1993), 102–120.

14. Maureen Duffy, *The Passionate Shepherdess: Aphra Behn 1640–89* (1977; re-print, New York: Methuen Press, 1989), 275; George Guffey, "Aphra Behn's *Oroon-oko*: Occasion and Accomplishment," in George Guffey and Andrew Wright, *Two English Novelists: Aphra Behn and Anthony Trollope* (Los Angeles: University of California, William Andrews Clark Memorial Library, 1975), 3–41; Todd, *The Secret Life of Aphra Behn*; Laura Brown, "The Romance of Empire: *Oroonoko* and the Trade in Slaves," *Ends of Empire: Women in Early Eighteenth-Century England* (Ithaca: Cornell University Press, 1993), 55–63. Duffy, Guffey, and Todd make the connection between the novel and James II, Maria of Modena, and their heir (Todd links the political context to *The Widow Ranter* as well); Brown sees par-allels between *Oroonoko* and Charles I. See also Ferguson's "News from the New World." Ferguson argues that a royalist reading of *Oroonoko* and *The Widow Ranter* neglects the political ambiguities in these two works (153).

15. Joanna Lipking, "Confusing Matters: Searching the Backgrounds of *Oroon-oko*," *Aphra Behn Studies*, 260.

16. See Todd's *Secret Life*, 411–423. Todd argues that Behn's *Oroonoko* and *Widow Ranter* reflect the current "chaos" of England's politics.

17. See Susan J. Owen, *Restoration Theatre and Crisis* (Oxford: Clarendon Press, 1992).

18. Guffey, "Aphra Behn's *Oroonoko*," 15; Todd, *Secret Life*, 417.

19. Kathleen M. Brown, *Gender, Race, and Power in Colonial Virginia: Good Wives, Nasty Wenches, and Anxious Patriarchs* (Chapel Hill: University of North Carolina Press, 1996), 142.

20. Brown, *Gender, Race, and Power*, 143.

21. Ibid., 145.

22. Ibid., 149.

23. Ibid., 150.

24. Ibid., 151.

25. Ibid., 154.

26. Ibid., 155.

27. Ibid., 157.

28. Ibid., 158.

29. Ibid., 157, 158.

30. "Nathaniel Bacon Esqr His Manifesto Concerning the present Troubles in Virginia," C.O. I/37, fols. 178–179. Reprinted in Brown, *Gender, Race, and Power,* 158.

31. Brown, *Gender, Race, and Power,* 160.

32. Cf. Thomas Jefferson Wertenbaker, *Torchbearer of the Revolution: The Story of Bacon's Rebellion and Its Leader* (Princeton: Princeton University Press, 1940).

33. Wilcomb E. Washburn, *The Governor and the Rebel: A History of Bacon's Rebellion in Virginia,* Institute of Early American History and Culture at Williamsburg (Chapel Hill: University of North Carolina Press, 1967), 1.

34. Brown, *Gender, Race, and Power,* 162.

35. C.O. I/40, fol. 154. Reprinted in Brown, *Gender, Race, and Power,* 165.

36. Charles M. Andrews, ed., *Narratives of the Insurrections* (New York, 1915), 130. Reprinted in Brown, *Gender, Race, and Power,* 165.

37. Andrews, *Narratives,* 68–69. Reprinted in Brown, *Gender, Race, and Power,* 165.

38. Brown, *Gender, Race, and Power,* 166.

39. David Hawke, *The Colonial Experience* (Indianapolis, Ind.: Bobbs Merrill, 1966), 248.

40. Brown, *Gender, Race, and Power,* 174.

41. Ibid., 167.

42. Martha W. McCartney, "Cockacoeske, Queen of Pamunkey: Diplomat and Suzeraine," *Powhatan's Mantle: Indians in the Colonial Southeast,* ed. Peter H. Wood, Gregory A. Waselkov, and M. Thomas Hatley (Lincoln: University of Nebraska Press, 1989), 177.

43. McCartney, "Cockacoeske, Queen of Pamunkey," 185.

44. Ibid., 177–178.

45. Ibid., 179.

46. Brown, *Gender, Race, and Power,* 168–169.

47. Ibid., 170.

48. C.O. I/40, fols. 54–55. Reprinted in Brown, *Gender, Race, and Power,* 171.

49. Brown, *Gender, Race, and Power,* 171.

50. Ibid., 175.

51. Ibid., 180.

52. Behn probably drew her information from *Strange News From Virginia Being a Full and True Account of the Life and Death of Nathaniel Bacon Esquire, Who Was the Only Cause and Original of All the late Troubles in that Country* (London: W. Harris, 1677). Todd notes several other possible sources: *More News from Virginia, Being A True and Full Relation of All Occurrances in that Countrey, since the Death of Nath. Bacon with an Account of Thirteen Persons that Have Been*

*Tryed and Executed for Their Rebellion There* (1677); and *A True Narrative of the Rise, Progress, and Cessation of the Late Rebellion in Virginia* (1676), in her preface to *The Widdow Ranter, The Works of Aphra Behn*, vol. 7, ed. Janet Todd (Columbus: Ohio State University Press, 1996), 288.

53. McCartney, "Cockacoeske, Queen of Pamunkey," 179.

54. Aphra Behn, *The Widdow Ranter, or the History of Bacon in Virginia* (1690) in *The Works of Aphra Behn*, vol. 7, ed. Janet Todd (Columbus: Ohio State University Press, 1996). All references are from this edition; page and line numbers will be cited in the text.

55. Behn's critique of contemporary notions of female chastity and honor may be seen throughout her work.

56. Marjorie Garber, *Vested Interests: Cross-Dressing and Cultural Anxiety* (New York: Routledge Press, 1992), 17.

57. In addition, Ranter (an outspoken deviant woman) may stand-in symbolically for Behn herself as a woman writer. Indeed, Behn plays with the problematic of the need to wear a male identity in respect to claiming authority in her own writing in her Preface to *The Lucky Chance* (1687), and in the Prefix to *Sir Patient Fancy* (1678), for example. In " 'Good, Sweet, Honey, Sugar-Candied Reader'," Jessica Munns suggests that "as a woman writer, Behn had and did not have place and space to maneuver. The very fact of her literary activity grounded her authority, but it was an authority always open to attack on the grounds of her gender" (53). Ranter, like Behn herself, also lays claim to a male identity, and thus her sword may represent Behn's pen. Yet, paradoxically, while Behn makes Ranter the "winner" in the play (she wins her lover through the male disguise), her female counterpart, the native woman Semernia, is undone through male masking. Perhaps, then, *The Widow Ranter* critiques the codes of cultural restraint imposed upon women that are based on the oversimplified gender binary of male and female. Behn's play shows that "playing a man" cannot in itself dissolve (or resolve) the complex gender, racial, and class boundaries and constructs of the period.

## Afterword

1. In England, intermarriage was tolerated in the eighteenth century (within limits); in literature taking place in North American colonies, it was not. See Roxann Wheeler's, "The Complexion of Desire: Racial Ideology and Mid-Eighteenth-Century British Novels," in *Eighteenth-Century Studies* 23 (Spring 1999): 308–332.

# Index